Biography Today

Profiles
of People
of Interest
to Young
Readers

Volume 20
Issue 2
April 2011

Cherie D. Abbey
Managing Editor

Omnigraphics

P.O. Box 31-1640
Detroit, MI 48231-1640

Cherie D. Abbey, *Managing Editor*

Peggy Daniels, Joan Goldsworthy, and Diane Telgen, *Sketch Writers*

Allison A. Beckett and Mary Butler, *Research Staff*

* * *

Peter E. Ruffner, *Publisher*
Matthew P. Barbour, *Senior Vice President*

* * *

Elizabeth Collins, *Research and Permissions Coordinator*
Kevin M. Hayes, *Operations Manager*
Cherry Stockdale, *Permissions Assistant*

Shirley Amore, Martha Johns, and Kirk Kauffmann, *Administrative Staff*

Special thanks to Frederick G. Ruffner for creating this series.

Library of Congress Cataloging-in-Publication Data

Contents

Preface

Biography Today is a magazine designed and written for the young reader—ages 9 and above—and covers individuals that librarians and teachers tell us that young people want to know about most: entertainers, athletes, writers, illustrators, cartoonists, and political leaders.

The Plan of the Work

The publication was especially created to appeal to young readers in a format they can enjoy reading and readily understand. Each issue contains approximately 10 sketches arranged alphabetically. Each entry provides at least one picture of the individual profiled, and boldfaced rubrics lead the reader to information on birth, youth, early memories, education, first jobs, marriage and family, career highlights, memorable experiences, hobbies, and honors and awards. Each of the entries ends with a list of easily accessible sources designed to lead the student to further reading on the individual and a current address. Retrospective entries are also included, written to provide a perspective on the individual's entire career.

Biographies are prepared by Omnigraphics editors after extensive research, utilizing the most current materials available. Those sources that are generally available to students appear in the list of further reading at the end of the sketch.

Indexes

Cumulative indexes are an important component of *Biography Today*. Each issue of the *Biography Today* General Series includes a Cumulative Names Index, which comprises all individuals profiled in *Biography Today* since the series began in 1992. In addition, we compile three other indexes: the Cumulative General Index, Places of Birth Index, and Birthday Index. See our web site, www.biographytoday.com, for these three indexes, along with the Names Index. All *Biography Today* indexes are cumulative, including all individuals profiled in both the General Series and the Subject Series.

Our Advisors

This series was reviewed by an Advisory Board comprising librarians, children's literature specialists, and reading instructors to ensure that the concept of this publication—to provide a readable and accessible biographical magazine for young readers—was on target. They evaluated the title as it developed, and their suggestions have proved invaluable. Any errors, however, are ours alone. We'd like to list the Advisory Board members and to thank them for their efforts.

Gail Beaver
Adjunct Lecturer
University of Michigan
Ann Arbor, MI

Cindy Cares
Youth Services Librarian
Southfield Public Library
Southfield, MI

Carol A. Doll
School of Information Science and Policy
University of Albany, SUNY
Albany, NY

Kathleen Hayes-Parvin
Language Arts Teacher
Birney Middle School
Southfield, MI

Karen Imarisio
Assistant Head of Adult Services
Bloomfield Twp. Public Library
Bloomfield Hills, MI

Rosemary Orlando
Director
St. Clair Shores Public Library
St. Clair Shores, MI

Our Advisory Board stressed to us that we should not shy away from controversial or unconventional people in our profiles, and we have tried to follow their advice. The Advisory Board also mentioned that the sketches might be useful in reluctant reader and adult literacy programs, and we would value any comments librarians might have about the suitability of our magazine for those purposes.

Your Comments Are Welcome

Our goal is to be accurate and up to date, to give young readers information they can learn from and enjoy. Now we want to know what you think. Take a look at this issue of *Biography Today*, on approval. Contact me with your comments. We want to provide an excellent source of biographical information for young people. Let us know how you think we're doing.

Cherie Abbey
Managing Editor, *Biography Today*
Omnigraphics, Inc.
P.O. Box 31-1640
Detroit, MI 48231-1640
www.omnigraphics.com
editorial@omnigraphics.com

Congratulations!

Congratulations to the following individuals and libraries who are receiving a free copy of *Biography Today,* Vol. 20, No. 2, for suggesting people who appear in this issue.

Amie Flora, Knox Middle School, Knox, TN

Mikayla

Mimy Poon, San Lorenzo, CA

Owen V., McKenna Elementary School, Massapequa, NY

Robert Bullard 1946-

American Sociologist and Environmental Justice Activist

Author of Numerous Books including *Dumping in Dixie: Race, Class and Environmental Quality*

Director of the Environmental Justice Resource Center at Clark Atlanta University

BIRTH

Robert Doyle Bullard was born on December 21, 1946, in Elba, Alabama. His father, Nehemiah Bullard, was a laborer. His mother, Myrtle Bullard, was a homemaker. Bullard is the fourth of five children. He has three brothers, Joe, Jimmy, and Leon, and one sister, Bettye.

YOUTH

Bullard grew up in an environment of strict racial segregation that was enforced throughout much of the southern U.S. at that time. Bullard explained, "I grew up in the all-black Mulberry Heights neighborhood located in Elba, Alabama. Elba was a typical southern small town with rigid racial boundaries where blacks and whites seldom interacted—except in a work setting. In the 1950s and 1960s, nearly every aspect of life in this small town was separate or segregated, including the public schools, parks, playgrounds and swimming pools, and libraries. The local public library was for 'whites only.' Our 'black library' was located at the segregated high school—that closed at 3:00 PM."

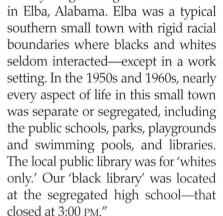

"I grew up in the all-black Mulberry Heights neighborhood located in Elba, Alabama. Elba was a typical southern small town with rigid racial boundaries where blacks and whites seldom interacted," Bullard recalled. "Nearly every aspect of life in this small town was separate or segregated, including the public schools, parks, playgrounds and swimming pools, and libraries. The local public library was for 'whites only.'"

This system of racial discrimination and the laws that enforced it were known as "Jim Crow." Under Jim Crow, African Americans were treated as second-class citizens. Bullard's childhood experiences with Jim Crow made him aware of how a person's race affected their access to housing, education, jobs, and transportation. Later in his life, Bullard drew upon his early experiences to understand how American communities grew and developed over time. "My upbringings did not shelter me from the fact that all societies are not created equal, [including] access to paved roads, sewer, and water. Nobody had to get me a movie ticket to see this. I saw it with my own eyes. And some of this exists today, the residual of Jim Crow in southern rural communities.

"I think growing up in the Jim Crow South, during a period in our nation's history where African Americans were largely judged as not equally qualified, made me want to excel and do more than 'average.' My parents always instilled in me and my siblings that we should never strive to be 'equal,' but we should strive to be 'better' and have that 'extra edge' that will set us apart from the pack," Bullard said. "My parents made sure my siblings and I had lots of books and magazines to read. They were strong believers in education and reading. Not being able to enter the Elba Library or check out a book did not stop me from writing 15 books." In fact, reading and writing were among Bullard's favorite things to do when he was young.

As a child, Bullard also enjoyed hiking, camping, and being outdoors. "I did not have video games or computers growing up," he recalled. "Most of my recreation and fun activities were outside—even in the heat of South Alabama. My parents always had a vegetable garden and fruit orchard which I enjoyed working and watching the plants grow and mature."

EDUCATION

Throughout school, Bullard's favorite subjects were history, government, geography, and English composition. He particularly enjoyed assignments that involved writing.

Bullard attended Alabama Agricultural and Mechanical University (Alabama A&M), where he studied history, government, and sociology. (Sociology is the study of human society and social systems such as culture, class, and race relations.) He earned a master's degree in sociology from Atlanta University (now Clark Atlanta University) and a doctorate degree (PhD) in sociology from Iowa State University.

CAREER HIGHLIGHTS

Over the course of a career spanning more than 30 years, Bullard has become known as the father of the environmental justice movement. Environmental justice is the equal right of all people to enjoy a safe and healthy place to live, work, and play. Environmental justice is based on the idea that environmental activists should be interested in the living conditions of people in cities in addition to protecting and conserving nature. As Bullard explained, "Environmental justice incorporates the idea that we are just as much concerned about wetlands, birds, and wilderness areas, but we're also concerned with urban habitats, where people live in cities, about reservations, about things that are happening along the U.S.-Mexican border, about children that are being poisoned by lead in housing and kids playing outside in contaminated playgrounds."

The area near the Shell Refinery in Norco, Louisiana, known as Cancer Alley, was one example of environmental problems in poor neighborhoods. Some homes were only 12 feet from the refinery, and many residents developed respiratory problems. According to Bullard, "The playgrounds in Norco, La., in Cancer Alley, are across from a huge Shell refinery. You stay there 15 minutes and you can't breathe."

Bullard is a pioneer in the fields of environmental justice research, scholarship, and activism. He sees no difference between the fight against racism and the fight for environmental protection. He is the author of many books on topics like environmental racism, industrial pollution, unfair land use, and unequal access to safe housing, transportation, and jobs. His work brings attention to the fact that poor minorities suffer the most from the world's environmental problems.

Many of Bullard's studies and reports have shown that racial segregation has resulted in hazardous waste sites being located in minority communities. "Environmental justice really is based on the premise that no community should become the dumping ground for things other people don't want.... We all produce garbage, but we all don't live next to a garbage dump," Bullard said. "You don't have to be a rocket scientist to understand that rich people throw away more than poor people, yet the poor get the burden and health risks of living near the landfills."

Getting Started

Before getting involved in environmental justice, Bullard worked as an urban planner. Urban planning is the design of cities and towns, including public spaces, business and residential areas, parks and recreation spaces, and roads. In 1978, he became an assistant professor of sociology at Texas Southern University in Houston. He intended to teach part-time while also conducting research in sociology.

By that time, Bullard decided that he wanted to model his career after W.E.B. Du Bois, an African-American civil rights activist, sociologist, historian, and author. "From my earliest moments in academia, I wanted to make sure I kept my feet grounded in the community while publishing in mainstream journals and cutting-edge publications that ... looked at racism and African Americans. I wanted to make sure my research was used, like Du Bois's, and that it pushed the envelope, whether it was smart growth, transportation, or housing."

Bullard's career in environmental justice began somewhat unexpectedly. His wife at that time, Linda McKeever Bullard, was an attorney. She asked Bullard to work on research for an important legal case against the creation of a city garbage dump in the middle of an African-American neighborhood in Houston called Northwood Manor. He agreed.

Bullard was surprised by the results of his research. "My students and I found that 100 percent of city-owned landfills in Houston were located in predominantly black neighborhoods, even though African Americans accounted for only 25 percent of the population. I expanded that research to include the entire southern United States," he remembered. "I got hooked. I started connecting the dots in terms of housing, residential patterns, patterns of land use, where highways go, where transportation routes go, and how economic development decisions are made. It was very clear that people who were making decisions—county commissioners or industrial boards or city councils—were not the same people who were 'hosting' these facilities in their communities. Without a doubt, it was a form of apartheid where whites were making decisions and black people and brown people and people of color, including Native Americans on reservations, had no seat at the table."

Bullard credits his ex-wife as "the single most important person that set me on the three-decade path of environmental justice. Although we did not live in Northwood Manor, Linda and I both felt assaulted by what was being proposed and by the discriminatory waste facility siting pattern that occurred over the previous five decades—with African-American Houston neighborhoods [getting] the bulk of the city's garbage.

"Even when you control for how much money people make and the price of housing, race still comes out as the number one factor in determining

13

THIRD EDITION

DUMPING

SAY NO T[...]

SHINTECH

OUR LIVES ARE NOT FOR SALE

DANGER CHEMICA[...]

IN DIXIE

Race, Class, and
Environmental Quality

Robert D. Bullard

Bullard's 1990 book Dumping in Dixie *became a groundbreaking work
in the new field of environmental justice.*

where toxic facilities are located," Bullard stressed. "Race permeates everything, in terms of housing, education, where people can live, land-use decisions, transportation, and mobility. And often, the fact that so many people of color live near facilities that other people don't want is based on historical factors that resulted in residential segregation and affected the decisions of housing commissions."

The 1979 lawsuit *Bean v. Southwestern Waste Management Corp.* was the first to use the 1964 Civil Rights Act to fight environmental discrimination in the location of a waste facility. "We made that connection," Bullard claimed. "You have a right to breathe clean air, you have a right to drink clean water, you have a right for your food not to be poisoned—just as you have a right to fair employment and equal opportunities in education."

Creating a National Movement

By the early 1980s, a national environmental justice movement was taking shape. In 1982, an organized protest against the creation of a hazardous waste dump in Warren County, North Carolina, brought renewed attention to the existence of environmental racism. The dump was to be located in a mostly African-American rural community. Members of the community were united in their opposition to the plan, and they staged a dramatic public protest to stop it. "The Warren County case brought home the 'in-your-face' politics of waste facility siting in the nation," Bullard declared. "The people said, 'No.' But more important, over 500 people went to jail trying to keep this dump out of the black community. Young school children, old people, and people from all walks of life put their bodies in front of dump trucks to protect their community."

In 1990, Bullard published *Dumping in Dixie: Race, Class, and Environmental Quality.* In this groundbreaking book, he documented disturbing trends in waste facility location throughout the U.S. and includes a call to action for environmental activists. It is widely regarded as the first publication to fully explain the concept of environmental justice. *Dumping in Dixie* was generally praised by critics, with a review in *Contemporary Sociology* calling it "provocative and helpful." In recognition of his pioneering work, the National Wildlife Foundation honored Bullard with a Conservation Achievement Award.

In 1991, Bullard helped to organize the first National People of Color Environmental Leadership Summit in Washington, DC. This event brought together representatives from more than 300 different organizations in the U.S., Puerto Rico, Canada, and Mexico. The goal was to unite people of color to work on issues related to environmental and economic justice, civil rights, and health. According to Bullard, "Out of this summit came 17 principles of environmental justice that laid the framework for how we would work together among ourselves, with grassroots groups, networks, and how we would relate to the national environmental groups."

Bullard's research and activism during these years resulted in significant changes to U.S. federal government operations. In 1991, the U.S. Environmental Protection Agency (EPA) Office of Environmental Equity was created. This office focused on environmental justice issues and produced the influential report "Environmental Equity: Reducing Risks for All Communities." Then President Bill Clinton expanded the EPA's Office of Environmental Justice and created the National Environmental Justice Advisory Council. In 1994, President Clinton signed an executive order to address environmental injustice in federal laws related to civil rights and environmental issues. Bullard was invited to the White House to witness the signing of this historic order.

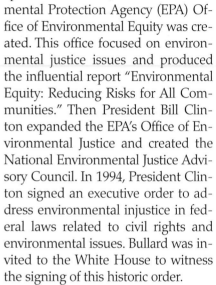

"*Environmental justice really is based on the premise that no community should become the dumping ground for things other people don't want.... We all produce garbage, but we all don't live next to a garbage dump,*" Bullard said. "*You don't have to be a rocket scientist to understand that rich people throw away more than poor people, yet the poor get the burden and health risks of living near the landfills.*"

Environmental Justice Resource Center

By 1994, Bullard was teaching sociology at Clark Atlanta University in Georgia. There he founded the Environmental Justice Resource Center to organize and inform activists. The Environmental Justice Resource Center presents environmental protection as a civil rights and social justice issue that affects people of color and low-income communities more than others. "We have to work even harder to hold the ground," Bullard said, "and for the notion that equal justice is for all communities and that we're all created equal."

Through the Environmental Justice Resource Center, Bullard was able to raise awareness of the many ways that environmental problems affect every part of life. His extensive research and analysis of waste facility loca-

Bullard shown in his office at Clark Atlanta University with enlarged covers of two of his books. He has written and edited books on several topics related to environmental justice, including Atlanta's public transit system policies.

tion decisions, environmental laws, regulations, and public policies revealed that these environmental problems tended to accumulate over time. Once a waste facility was located in a particular community, it became easier to place another one there, and then another. The combined effect of multiple facilities in one area is devastating.

Bullard explained the hazards of these multiple problems like this: "It's not just the landfill, it's not just the incinerator, it's not just the garbage dump, it's not just the crisscrossing freeway and highway, and the bus barns that dump all that stuff in these neighborhoods—it's all that combined. Even if each particular facility is in compliance, there are no regulations that take into account this saturation. It may be legal, but it is immoral. Just like slavery was legal, but slavery has always been immoral.

"Whether it's by design, or whether it's by default, or whether it's by accident, the negative health impacts are the same. So we're not even arguing about the intentionality anymore. What we're saying is, if a kid is being impacted by lead, or by industrial pollution, or whatever—whether the community was there first or the plant was there first, the kid can be just as sick. So that should not be an argument. The good question is, 'What are we going to do about it?'"

The Environmental Justice Resource Center also highlights issues of race and class in environmental decision-making. "We strongly believe that people of color must speak for themselves and do for themselves," Bullard

17

explained. "We are seeing an increase in the number of grassroots people of color environmental and economic justice groups emerge across the U.S., Puerto Rico, Canada, and Mexico. This is also the case in the Caribbean, Latin America, Asia, and Africa. Trans-boundary and international collaborations are forming among nongovernmental organizations to address global human rights, environmental, and economic justice issues." In this way, environmental justice has become a global issue.

"You have a right to breathe clean air, you have a right to drink clean water, you have a right for your food not to be poisoned—just as you have a right to fair employment and equal opportunities in education."

In the years since founding the Environmental Justice Resource Center, Bullard has made tremendous progress in raising awareness of the relationship between civil rights and environmentalism. Bringing civil rights and environmental activists together produces benefits across many different parts of modern society. "The environmental justice movement has basically redefined what environmentalism is all about," he explained. "It basically says that the environment is everything: where we live, work, play, go to school, as well as the physical and natural world. And so we can't separate the physical environment from the cultural environment. We have to talk about making sure that justice is integrated throughout all of the stuff that we do.

"A lot has changed in 20 years," Bullard observed. "We have strong regional and ethnic-based environmental justice networks and grassroots groups. We have an array of environmental justice courses being taught at colleges and universities all across the country. Several law schools have legal clinics that work on [environmental justice] issues. We even have four university-based environmental justice centers. We have made a lot of progress. But we still have a lot of work to do."

Future Plans

While some progress has been made, Bullard notes that race is still the biggest factor in the location of hazardous waste sites. In 2007, his research showed that more than half of the nine million people living within two miles of U.S. hazardous waste facilities were minorities. "Environmental racism is alive and well. Racism is making some of us sick—mentally and physically.... Where you live can impact your quality of life. In the real

Bullard has been active in many human rights causes, including this 2005 march in Atlanta, Georgia, to commemorate the 40th anniversary of the Voting Rights Act.

world, all communities are not created equal. Blacks, whether rural, urban, or suburban, are more likely than whites to live in polluted environments, and lack health insurance and access to health care. In general, black communities receive less environmental protection than white communities."

As a result, Bullard has no plans to stop working on issues related to environmental justice. His focus remains on empowering people to create change and to work for safe, healthy communities. "Our communities are under siege. These threats are real—not imagined. All you have to do is turn on the television or read the newspaper and the reality hits home loud and clear," Bullard declared. He has a clear idea of what will be required in the future. "As a group, black people need a laser-like focus on such issues as environmental and economic justice, public health, livable communities, pollution prevention, brownfields redevelopment, clean production, transportation, air quality, and urban sprawl just to name a few areas."

Bullard also sees a need for more young people to join the environmental justice movement. A new generation of leaders is needed. "Young people should understand that every successful social movement in this country has had a youth and student component. This was true for the civil rights movement, women's movement, anti-war movement, environmental movement, and others. Movements need young people to grow and

19

thrive. Young people must be educated, trained, and mentored to take over the leadership reigns from the elders."

In particular, Bullard would like to see more young people of color working on environmental justice issues. "It's a great field. The opportunities are unlimited," he remarked. "It's an area where you can have not only a great career, but a great impact. The latter is where a legacy can be left. The field is growing and advancing. It's important that minority students have a significant stake in what happens in communities of color—not to say that every black student lives in a black neighborhood—but you can have an impact, whether on a reservation, a barrio, or an ethnic enclave.… We have to be researchers and advance the field, but if you can get elected to office or direct an environmental office—government or organization—you can contribute beyond the individual level and have a huge impact.

"The best advice I have for young people is to set your sights on a goal you would like to achieve and work hard to get there. Do not let anyone tell you or convince you that you can't excel. Set your sights high," Bullard said. "There is nothing you can't achieve if you set your mind to it. Most of the people who have made advancements in our society were not 'sprinters' [work for short term] but were 'marathon runners' [work for the long term]. In the struggle for environmental justice, we need more young people who are willing to be marathon runners."

MAJOR INFLUENCES

Bullard has many personal heroes and people who have inspired him. At the top of the list are his parents. He also counts his grandmother among those who have had a big impact on his life. Bullard described his grandmother as "a strong advocate of education, of standing on your own two feet and not letting anybody ride your back. She instilled that in me, in my father, and my parents also instilled it in me."

In addition, Bullard said, "Educators, scholars, and activists have always been a big hit with me!" He named W.E.B. Du Bois as "the number one intellectual, scholar, teacher, researcher, and political activist who has influenced my academic career." Bullard has expressed admiration for many African-American leaders from the past: civil rights leader Martin Luther King Jr., religious leader and activist Malcolm X, voting rights activist and civil rights leader Fannie Lou Hamer, and writer, speaker, social reformer, and anti-slavery activist Frederick Douglass. "The people who came before me … really combined telling the truth and not letting things come back and get you—repercussions—just because you're standing for social justice."

MARRIAGE AND FAMILY

Bullard was married to Linda McKeever Bullard, an attorney. The marriage ended in divorce.

HOBBIES AND OTHER INTERESTS

Bullard enjoys gardening in his spare time.

SELECTED WRITINGS

Books

Dumping in Dixie: Race, Class, and Environmental Quality, 1990

Sprawl City: Race, Politics, and Planning in Atlanta, 2000 (editor, with Glenn S. Johnson and Angel O. Torres)

Highway Robbery: Transportation Racism, New Routes to Equity, 2004 (editor, with Glenn S. Johnson and Angel O. Torres)

The Quest for Environmental Justice: Human Rights and the Politics of Pollution, 2005

Growing Smarter: Achieving Livable Communities, Environmental Justice, and Regional Equity, 2007

Race, Place, and Environmental Justice after Hurricane Katrina: Struggles to Reclaim, Rebuild, and Revitalize New Orleans and the Gulf Coast, 2009

Environmental Health and Racial Equity in the United States: Strategies for Building Environmentally Just, Sustainable, and Livable Communities, forthcoming

Periodicals

"Victims of Their Environment," *Atlanta Journal and Constitution*, Jan. 19, 1995, p.A11

"It's Not Just, Pollution," *Our Planet*, Sep. 2001

"Toxic Waste Dumpers Prefer to Poison Poor People," *Atlanta Journal and Constitution*, Nov. 28, 2002

"Environmental Justice for All," *New Crisis*, Jan./Feb. 2003, p.24

"The Color of Toxic Debris," *The American Prospect*, Mar. 2009, p.A9

HONORS AND AWARDS

Conservation Achievement Award (National Wildlife Foundation): 1990

CNN People You Should Know (CNN): 2007

Environmental Leaders of the Century (Newsweek): 2008

100 History Makers in the Making (TheGrio.com): 2010

FURTHER READING

Periodicals

Atlanta Magazine, Mar. 2007
E: the Environmental Magazine, July/Aug. 1998, p.10
Earth First! Journal, July 1999
National Catholic Reporter, June 16, 2006, p.A2
Sierra, Nov./Dec. 2005, p.28
Smithsonian, June 2008, p.33

Online Articles

http://www.ejrc.cau.edu
   (Environmental Justice Resource Center, "Robert Bullard," undated;
   "Why Blacks Should Be Concerned About the Environment: An Interview with Dr. Robert Bullard," Nov. 1999)
http://www.greenamerica.org/pubs/caq/articles/Fall2007/robertbullard.cfm
   (Green America, "Our Interview with Robert Bullard," Fall 2007)
http://www.grist.org
   (Grist, "Meet Robert Bullard, the Father of Environmental Justice," Mar.
   14, 2006)
http://www.sptimes.com/2007/09/09/Opinion/The_world_s_a_dirty_p.shtml
   (St. Petersburg Times, "The World's a Dirty Place When You Are Poor,"
   Sep. 9, 2007)
http://www.thegrio.com/black-history/thegrios-100/thegrios-100-robert-
   bullard.php
   (TheGrio.com, "TheGrio's 100: Robert Bullard, Father of Environmental
   Justice Inspires Next Generation," Feb. 2, 2010)

ADDRESS

Robert Bullard
Environmental Justice Resource Center
Clark Atlanta University
223 James P. Brawley Drive
Atlanta, GA 30314

WORLD WIDE WEB SITE

http://ejrc.cau.edu

Paula Creamer 1986-

American Golfer
Winner of the 2010 U.S. Women's Open

BIRTH

Paula Creamer was born on August 5, 1986, in Mountain View, California, and raised in Pleasanton, California. Both towns are near San Francisco. She is the only child of Paul Creamer, a commercial airline pilot and former Navy pilot, and Karen Creamer.

YOUTH

As a young child, Creamer enjoyed gymnastics, but she didn't have the ideal body type for the sport. "I was too tall for the bars and the beam," she remarked. "I really just did floor exercises. I later became an acrobatic dancer.... I was good. We traveled all over and won lots of big events." One day while attempting an acrobatic trick, Creamer took a bad fall. "I landed on my neck, and I heard something crack and pop, and I thought I was paralyzed," she remembered. Although she wasn't seriously injured, thoughts of that fall haunted her. "It was never really the same," she said. "I didn't like tumbling anymore. Then I found golf, and it was a blessing."

Creamer's father golfed, and the family lived next to the Castlewood Country Club, where there are two championship golf courses and an excellent youth golf program. Her father introduced her to the basics of the game when she was 10 years old. It was obvious she was naturally talented, and she liked it immediately. "I had great teachers who made it fun," she recalled. Her average score quickly dropped from 90 to the low 80s and then the low 70s. (The object of golf is to get the ball in the hole with as few strokes as possible, and the total number of strokes is the player's final score.) By the age of 11, Creamer had won 18 junior tournaments.

EDUCATION

Creamer's education was a bit unusual. She became intrigued with the Leadbetter Academy in Bradenton, Florida, which specializes in developing talented young golfers. She convinced her parents to take her there for a visit and some instruction. "I thought it was the most unbelievable place," she said. "Leaving, I was so depressed because I wanted to stay." In 2000, the whole family relocated so she could attend Leadbetter full-time. "It was like a fairy tale. It has everything you need to become the player you want to be. You aren't forced to do anything; it's up to you. It has physical fitness, media training, and mental training," she said. Creamer also attended the Pendleton School, a private school attended by many elite young athletes who train in the area. She graduated from Pendleton in 2005.

GOLF SCORING

In golf scoring, players keep track of how many "strokes" it takes them to hit the ball from the tee to the cup; the fewer strokes, the better. "Par" refers to the standard number of strokes it should take a player to complete each hole. For example, most golf courses include short holes, which are usually designated as "par 3," as well as longer holes, which are designated as "par 5." On a regulation, 18-hole golf course, par for all holes will add up to 72.

On the professional golf circuit, most tournaments take place over four days. Each day, all the players shoot one "round" of 18 holes. After the first two rounds, they often cut the field to the top 60 or 70 golfers (players either "make the cut" or "miss the cut"). After all four rounds, the scores are totaled and the player with the lowest score wins the tournament. This format is called "stroke play." There are many tournaments on the women's professional golf tour, but the most prestigious are the four major, or "Grand Slam," events: the Kraft Nabisco Championship, the LPGA Championship, the U.S. Women's Open, and the Women's British Open.

Many amateur tournaments and team tournaments (like the Solheim Cup) use a different scoring system, called "match play." In this system, golfers play one-on-one over 18 holes. Whoever takes the fewest strokes on a hole scores a single point; if the two golfers tie they split the point. They keep a running tally of holes; if Player A has won 5 holes and Player B has won 3 holes, Player A is considered "2 up." A match can end before 18 holes if one player mathematically eliminates the other. In this case, the final score is listed as two numbers: the first indicating how many up the winner was, the second showing how many holes were left over. The highest winning score in match play is thus "10-and-8," meaning the winner won the first 10 holes, so they did not need to play the last eight. If a round of 18 holes ends in a tie, the match goes to "sudden death" on extra holes—meaning that the first player to win a hole wins the match.

"The Pink Panther"

While Creamer was a student at Leadbetter, one of her friends gave her the nickname the Pink Panther, after the all-pink cartoon character of the same name. Pink outfits and accessories are her trademark, both on and off the golf course. "I've always loved pink," she explained. "I love how feminine it is, and at the same time it's kind of a power color." She also gained a reputation as a fierce competitor, intensely focused on her game.

While attending Pendleton and Leadbetter, Creamer competed at the highest levels of amateur and junior golf. She won 19 national tournaments as an amateur, including 11 sanctioned by the American Junior Golf Association (AJGA). In 2002, she was part of the winning U.S. team in the Junior Solheim Cup, one of the most prestigious events in junior golf.

CAREER HIGHLIGHTS

Outstanding Amateur

Creamer's 2003 season was one of the most outstanding ever played by an amateur golfer, male or female. She won seven junior tournaments and made the semifinals for two major competitions, the U.S. Girls' Junior and the U.S. Women's Amateur. If they qualify, amateur golfers can play in a limited number of events on the professional golf tour run by the Ladies Professional Golf Association (LPGA). Creamer qualified for the U.S. Women's Open, but she did not make the cut to play in the final round. She did make the cut in two other LPGA competitions, however. She also played at the Junior Solheim again that year, and the U.S. took second in the event. At the end of the season, she was named Player of the Year by the American Junior Golf Association and Junior Player of the Year by *Golfweek* and *Golf Digest*. That year also saw an important improvement in her game. She was already impressive at hitting the ball off the tee, and she knew how to keep her cool even when playing a high-stakes game. Her weakness was her "short game," the shots taken close to or on the green. To reach the level of play that would take her to the top of competition, Creamer needed to sharpen her short game, and she did.

Creamer had another impressive year in 2004. In March, she played in the Kraft Nabisco Championship, one of the four "majors" in women's golf. Sponsors of tournaments can invite promising players to take part, paying their entry fees as well. This is known as a "sponsor's exemption." Creamer had a sponsor's exemption for the Kraft Nabisco, and she tied for the 45th spot in the final standings.

The Kraft Nabisco was an important turning point for Creamer. Being on the course with older players she admired, she found herself feeling starstruck, rather than focusing on playing her best game. That showed in her higher scores. "I had to get stronger," she recalled. "But mentally that was a big thing to overcome, to believe in myself and be able to compete at that level." She worked hard to change her attitude before her next event, the

Creamer made the semifinals at the U.S. Women's Amateur during her outstanding 2003 season, when she was just 17.

ShopRite LPGA Classic in Abescon, New Jersey. She finished second, losing to Cristie Kerr by just one shot on the final hole.

Creamer continued to play strongly in 2004 and was chosen for the U.S. team for the 33rd Curtis Cup. Held every other year, the two-day tournament is the greatest prize in the world of women's international amateur golf. In 2004, the U.S. team was the youngest in the history of the event, with five teens on the squad and no player over the age of 25. The U.S. won, defeating Ireland and Great Britain. Creamer's 2-0 victory over Emma Duggleby of England in the singles division was a strong contribution to the team's overall performance.

One of Creamer's teammates was Michelle Wie, a talented golfer from Hawaii who was only 14 at the time. The two already had a rivalry on the golf course, but they became friends while on the Curtis Cup team. "When we were off the golf course, we didn't talk about golf," Creamer said. "I love shopping and fashion, and she loves it, too. We have a lot in common. We were on the plane, drawing outfits and designing clothes."

Creamer competed in seven LPGA tour events in 2004, usually playing on sponsor's exemptions, and she made the cut in every one. In addition to her fine performances in the ShopRite and the Curtis Cup, she finished 13th in the U.S. Women's Open. She and Wie tied with the best amateur scores in the event. Creamer was 18th in the Canadian Women's Open, and she went to the World Amateur Team Championship as part of the U.S. squad, which took second place. Her 2004 season earned her the Nancy Lopez Award from the LPGA, given each year to the best amateur in women's golf.

Turning Pro

The difference between amateur and professional status is important in golf. Amateurs can only accept a limited amount of prize money each year. If they break this rule, they can have their amateur status taken away. Most professional golfers earn their living by teaching golf, but the top players can qualify to play in major tours sponsored by the LPGA, the Professional Golf Association (PGA), and other organizations. Talented junior golfers usually continue to play as amateurs during college before deciding whether or not to turn pro. A golfer as talented as Creamer, however, might qualify for the pro tour without playing first for a college team.

In 2004, Creamer took part in the LPGA Qualifying School, a series of tournaments that is also known as "Q-School." Those who prove them-

Creamer's dominating play at the 2004 Daytona Beach LPGA Qualifying School (Q-School) earned her a spot on the pro tour.

selves in Q-School win a spot on the pro tour, but if things do not go well, participants may hold on to their amateur status. Creamer decided that if she didn't do well in Q-School, she would remain an amateur, enter college, and play collegiate golf. Her real desire was to win a spot on the pro tour, however. "I want to be the No. 1 player in the world," she stated in 2004. "And if I turn pro, I want to win my first year out there. Those are lofty goals, but I mean what I say, and I'm going to do everything I can do to get there."

Creamer dominated the 2004 Q-School. In December, at the LPGA final qualifying tournament in Daytona Beach, Florida, she became the youngest winner and the first amateur winner in the history of the event. Her victory was decisive—she took the final round by five strokes. Soon afterward, she declared herself a professional. She wrapped up her studies at Pendleton and joined the LPGA pro tour in February 2005, at age 18. "Going to college and getting your degree is so important. I wanted to experience that. I really did," she said. "[But] I wanted to be the No. 1 player in the world instead of the No. 1 collegiate player."

LPGA Rookie of the Year

Being part of the LPGA tour and having the opportunity to watch and play against so many other world-class players was an incredible learning experience for Creamer. Always goal-oriented, she first set her sights on qualifying for the Kraft Nabisco Championship, held late in March, one of the four majors. In 2004, she had played in the Kraft Nabisco on a sponsor's exemption. In 2005, she earned her way into the tournament by placing in the top 15 money-winners from the first three LPGA events of the season. She finished in a five-way tie for 19th place.

A few months later, Creamer became the youngest winner in the history of a multi-round LPGA event, triumphing in the Sybase Classic on May 23, 2005, just a few days before her official graduation from high school. Much of the final round was played in cold rain, and at one point, it seemed Creamer's game was falling apart, but she defeated Gloria Park and Jeong Jang by just one stroke. Two months after Sybase, she took the Evian Masters in France with an eight-shot win. That made her the youngest winner ever on the Ladies European Tour, and the prize money pushed her career earnings over the million-dollar mark. She was the youngest LPGA player to earn that much, and she had done so more quickly than any other player.

Creamer's rookie season had other highlights. She won twice on the Japanese LPGA tour and took third place at the LPGA Championship. She also qualified for a spot on the U.S. team for the Solheim Cup. Each year, the Solheim pits the top 12 U.S. players against the top 12 European players. Creamer was the youngest player ever to compete in the event, which the U.S. won that year. When the season ended, her rookie earnings stood at $1.5 million and she was ranked the second-best player on the LPGA tour.

It was not surprising when she was named the LPGA Rookie of the Year. This award is based on a point system, and Creamer stood more than 500 points ahead of her closest rival. "Paula has played incredibly well during her rookie year and has displayed poise and maturity beyond her years," said Carolyn Bivens, who was commissioner-elect of the LPGA at that time. "She has consistently played at the highest level and has set a new performance standard for rookies."

Injuries and Experience

Being a top-ranked pro golfer presented new challenges. Creamer's schedule was hectic. Professional events are held more frequently than amateur events, leaving less time for practice. She faced the distractions of celebrity parties and endorsement deals with many companies, including Kraft, TaylorMade, Adidas, and Bridgestone. She also sprained ligaments in her hand in 2006. She went without a win that year, and her ranking fell to 11th.

In 2007, Creamer had two LPGA wins and was part of the U.S. Team for the Solheim Cup. She made the winning stroke for the Americans in the final round at the Solheim. Her LPGA ranking rebounded to third that year. The 2008 season saw further improvement. She won four times on the tour, earned $1.8 million in prize money, and set a course record score of 60 while winning the Jamie Farr Owens Corning Classic in Sylvania, Ohio. At the end of the season, she was once again ranked the second-best player in the LPGA.

Asked if she regretted not attending college, Creamer said, "No. I can honestly say that. These have been the best five years of my life. There is so much I want to do in women's golf and I'm living my dream.... I will go back and get my degree, there's not a doubt in my mind. But when you have opportunities like I did, you have to take advantage of them.

As 2008 drew to a close, however, Creamer developed serious health problems that troubled her into the next year. During a trip to Mexico she suffered severe abdominal pain, but doctors didn't know what was wrong. Over the next months she endured pain, vomiting, weight loss, and weakness. She was tested for many different illnesses and tried different medications, but doctors were unable to determine the cause of the problems. Her weight went up and down, and her strength deteriorated. Minor illnesses became major because her body's immune system was weakened. Her health problems persisted the next year and at times forced her to withdraw from competition or play in pain. She had no wins in 2009, and her ranking fell to ninth. Her health eventually came back, although doctors still didn't know why. "They still have no idea what was wrong with me, which is a scary thought knowing that it could come back," Creamer acknowledged. Dealing with these health issues was difficult for her. "It was hard," she said of this period. "But I feel like it made me a lot stronger, mentally, and it put things in perspective. It was a year of learning."

Triumph in the 2010 U.S. Open

Creamer had high hopes for the 2010 season, but it had barely started when she was forced to withdraw from the LPGA Thailand event because

After several years battling illness, Creamer came back strongly in 2010, winning the U.S. Women's Open.

of a thumb injury. At the end of March, she underwent surgery on a damaged ligament. She thought she might have to take the whole season off, but her doctor let her return to play four months after surgery. It was the longest she had ever gone without playing golf since she had taken up the game. Even during her layoff, she was preparing mentally for the 65th U.S. Women's Open, to be held in July in Oakmont, Pennsylvania. She got back on the course just four weeks before the Open.

Creamer's performance over the four days of play in the Women's Open was commanding. She started the final round with a three-stroke lead and never fell below two shots. She won by four shots, with a final-round score of just 69. Her total score was 281, three under par. She played three sub-par rounds in a row, something accomplished only once before in Oakmont's history. Creamer had finally claimed her first victory in an LPGA majors. Due to her injury, she limited her play for the rest of the season, but she still finished with a ninth-place ranking and $875,140 in winnings.

Creamer describes herself as "energetic, cheerful, competitive, and determined." She loves golf and encourages children to get involved with it. "You learn so many lessons: control, adversity, time management, integrity, honesty. And you can have so much fun doing something you love. You can't beat that."

Asked in 2010 if she regretted not attending college, Creamer said, "No. I can honestly say that. These have been the best five years of my life. There is so much I want to do in women's golf and I'm living my dream…. I will go back and get my degree, there's not a doubt in my mind. But when you have opportunities like I did, you have to take advantage of them."

HOME AND FAMILY

Creamer lives in Isleworth, an exclusive community just outside Windermere, Florida, in the greater Orlando area. Isleworth includes a championship golf course, and many top golfers have homes there. In 2009, Creamer bought her own house, seven doors away from the one where her parents live. She says her focused and competitive nature are much like her father's.

HOBBIES AND OTHER INTERESTS

Creamer loves to get her hair done, get manicures, and go shopping. She enjoys getting dressed up and looking at the latest fashion trends. She has said that if she weren't devoted to golf, she would like to have a career in fashion design. She is also interested in nutrition and fitness.

Creamer also enjoys watching TV and movies. She likes the TV programs "America's Next Top Model," "Newlyweds," and "CSI." Her favorite golf movie is *Happy Gilmore.* Other favorite movies include *Shrek, Pretty Woman, Curly Sue,* and *Dirty Dancing.*

HONORS AND AWARDS

AJGA Player of the Year: 2003
Golf Digest Junior Player of the Year: 2003
Golfweek Junior Player of the Year: 2003
Golf Digest Amateur of the Year: 2004
Golfweek Amateur of the Year: 2004
LPGA Nancy Lopez Award: 2005

LPGA Rookie of the Year: 2005
U.S. Women's Open (LPGA): 2010

FURTHER READING

Periodicals

Golf Fitness, Nov.-Dec., 2008, p.14
Golf Digest, Jan. 2006, p.110
USA Today, Dec. 14, 2004, p.C3; June 28, 2006, p. C12

Online Articles

http://www.golfdigest.com
    (Golf Digest, "Interview with Paula Creamer," Mar. 1, 2010)

ADDRESS

Paula Creamer
c/o Jay Burton
IMG
1360 East 9th Street, Ste. 100
Cleveland, OH 44114

WORLD WIDE WEB SITES

http://www.lpga.com
http://twitter.thepcreamer.com

Lucas Cruikshank 1993-

American Actor, Writer, and Comedian
Creator of the Fictional Character Fred Figglehorn
Producer and Star of the Hit Web Video Series
"Fred" and the Film *Fred: The Movie*

BIRTH

Lucas Cruikshank was born on August 29, 1993, in Columbus,
Nebraska, a small rural town near Omaha. The fourth of eight
children, he has two brothers and five sisters. His father,
David, works as an engineer. His mother, Molly, is a nurse.

YOUTH

Cruikshank grew up in a farming community, in a house that was surrounded by cornfields on three sides. For as long as he can remember, he wanted to be an actor. He enjoyed putting on shows and performing with his brothers, sisters, and cousins during family vacations and other gatherings. Cruikshank's first videos were recordings of these performances. "I've been doing videos for as long as I can remember," he said. "I've always been messing around with cameras wherever I could find them. Whether it was my mom's camera or a friend's camera."

By the time he was nine years old, Cruikshank was downloading movie scripts from the Internet and acting out the stories. "I always had dreams of being an actor," he explained. "I had a really strong drive. I was looking online for auditions in Nebraska. I wanted to do it so bad." He found opportunities to act on stage with local theater groups. He appeared in productions of *High School Musical*, *Aladdin*, and *Grease*.

> *By the time he was nine years old, Cruikshank was downloading movie scripts from the Internet and acting out the stories. "I always had dreams of being an actor," he explained. "I had a really strong drive. I was looking online for auditions in Nebraska. I wanted to do it so bad."*

EDUCATION

Cruikshank attends Lakeview High School in Columbus, Nebraska. In addition to English, math, and science, he also studies Spanish, journalism, and drama. He has had the same classmates since the third grade. "I go to a really small, country school," he commented. "So I've been in school with them since third grade. They all know me as the same Lucas before the YouTube videos took off."

Cruikshank's parents support his dream of a career in acting, though they have insisted that school must come first. Even with the growing popularity of his videos and other projects, he is realistic about the importance of his education. "My parents obviously always have school come first," he stated. "I have to do my homework before I can do any of the other stuff with Fred. It's not that big of a deal." After graduating, Cruikshank plans to go to college to study drama and writing.

Cruikshank as Fred Figglehorn.

CAREER HIGHLIGHTS

By the time he was a teenager, Cruikshank had developed a reputation as a successful entertainer of children and teens. He is the writer, producer, director, and star of the popular Web video series "Fred," which has attracted one of the biggest groups of viewers on YouTube. The "Fred" video series documents the life, adventures, and mishaps of Fred Figglehorn, a fictional character created and performed by Cruikshank. "Fred" began as a hobby that Cruikshank thought would be just for fun. But within just four years, "Fred" grew into an entertainment phenomenon that includes the original video series, a full-length movie, two albums of music, and a line of merchandise including clothing, stickers, posters, and mugs. The "Fred" YouTube channel was the first ever to reach one million subscribers.

Creating Fred Figglehorn

Cruikshank first got the idea for the character of Fred Figglehorn when he was 13 years old. "I got a digital video camera for my 13th birthday so I started making up these random characters," he recalled. "I just loved writing and acting. So I recorded a few videos with this camera and Fred was one of them."

Fred Figglehorn is a hyper, overexcited, loud-mouthed, fast-talking six-year-old with an annoying high-pitched voice. He loses his temper easily and yells about everything. Cruikshank uses digital video editing software to distort his own voice into Fred's trademark screech. He also speeds up the videos to make Fred appear even more frantic and agitated. Cruikshank explained that the inspiration for Fred came from watching his younger brothers. "They were crazy little kids, and I exaggerated what they did and made Fred like them."

In June 2006, Cruikshank uploaded the first Fred videos to YouTube. "YouTube was just being created when I was 13 and back then it was mostly just vloggers [video bloggers]," he said. "I thought it was so weird how people did that so Fred was kind of poking fun at that." Cruikshank thought it would be funny to create a fictional video blogger who was a little boy. The concept was that each video would feature Fred ranting to his webcam about the different things that were going on in his life.

Cruikshank originally created the videos for his friends and family members to enjoy. He was surprised when complete strangers began leaving comments on the Fred videos posted on YouTube. "I didn't really understand YouTube at the time," he admitted. "I didn't know that millions of people could watch your video. I just thought that the friends I sent it to could watch it. So I was really surprised when I posted 'Fred' and it totally blew up."

At that time, Cruikshank shared a YouTube channel called JKL Productions with two of his cousins. Each person contributed videos on different topics, most having nothing to do with Fred Figglehorn. Their collective channel soon began attracting a large number of viewers interested in seeing Fred's latest antics. YouTube soon offered the three cousins a partnership to place ads on the pages with the most viewers. At the height of its popularity, JKL Productions' ad revenue from YouTube averaged $2,000 each month.

The "Fred" Channel

In May 2007, Cruikshank created the "Fred" channel on YouTube and set a goal of posting a new Fred video every two to three weeks. By this time, he had created Fred's whole world. Although there was no real plot or much of an ongoing storyline to the video series, there was a cast of characters and a background story. Fred's mother struggles with alcoholism and the challenges of parenting while his father is in prison. Fred's only friend is geeky Bertha, and he nurtures a crush on his neighbor Judy, who is pretty and popular. None of these characters ever appears in the videos. Instead, viewers learn about Fred's world through the stories he tells to the camera.

"Fred" videos are based on simple ideas drawn from everyday life experiences. Some of the most popular videos include "Fred Goes Swimming," "Fred Goes to the Dentist," and "Fred Sees a Therapist." Cruikshank begins the process of making each video by first coming up with the title. He then develops a story outline for each title, but does not write anything before filming. "I know the general idea of what the video will be—beginning, middle, and end—and then from there, I pretty much [improvise] it. I've never really scripted anything with Fred." With only his ideas for what Fred will say and do, Cruikshank usually records each video in one try. He then edits the video and posts it online.

In creating each video, Cruikshank caters to his target audience of children and teens. He has attracted a loyal and devoted group of fans, although not everyone appreciates Fred's screechy voice and high-speed commentary. "It's an acquired taste," Cruikshank acknowledged. "I think the kids like it because it's funny, and they also like it because they could relate to the things that Fred goes through. Like, Fred doesn't have any friends, or maybe how he doesn't have a dad in his house, or something like that. So there's a lot of things you could relate to Fred. I think that adults, for the most part, hear the voice and automatically push it away, because it's so in your face. They don't really give it a chance."

Cruikshank was surprised when complete strangers began leaving comments on the Fred videos posted on YouTube. "I didn't really understand YouTube at the time," he admitted. "I didn't know that millions of people could watch your video. I just thought that the friends I sent it to could watch it. So I was really surprised when I posted 'Fred' and it totally blew up."

Response to "Fred"

Response to "Fred" has included both positive and negative reactions. The video series has gotten many hateful comments from YouTube viewers, but Cruikshank ignores the negativity. "I think online, like on YouTube and stuff, people could pretty much say whatever they want. They have no filter in their brain, because no one knows who they are. They're totally anonymous, so they could say whatever they want. But when they're in person with me, they wouldn't say those things, because I can actually see who they are. They're not another name on a comments list."

Cruikshank appearing as Fred on an episode of "Hannah Montana," shown here with Emily Osment and Miley Cyrus.

Entertainment critics have praised Cruikshank's work even if they don't always understand Fred's appeal. A reviewer for *BusinessWeek* recognized Cruikshank's talent with the comment that "adults don't get it, kids can't get enough of it." A *Los Angeles Times* reviewer said that he "has more range than a parent might guess from the shrill voice emanating from the family computer," and concluded that "in the land of positive-message-laden kids TV, Fred is a force for giddy anarchy."

In response to the conflicting feedback from his admirers and detractors, Cruikshank said, "I really try not to focus on any of that—the comments, or the views, or the subscribers, or any of that. It kind of changes how you think. I'd rather just be thinking about the creative part of it."

The "Fred" Channel has become wildly and unexpectedly successful, gathering a huge number of subscribers and millions of viewers for each video. This success has created new opportunities for Cruikshank. He has appeared as a guest star on the popular television shows "iCarly" and "Hannah Montana." In 2009, he won the Teen Choice Award for Choice Web Star. Around the same time, he also created a line of Fred merchandise, and sold more than 800,000 T-shirts within one year. In addition, he released the CD *It's Hackin' Christmas with Fred* in 2009, containing four tracks: two original songs along with Fred's version of "Jingle Bells" and "The 12 Days of Christmas."

Fred: The Movie

With the explosive popularity of the "Fred" series, Cruikshank began getting offers for movies and television shows based on the character. At first he was reluctant to make any deals. "Lots of people came to me with ideas: they wanted to do a TV show, a movie, products. They wanted to make Fred mainstream. At first I was really leery because I was scared someone was going to get a hold of it and totally make it something it wasn't. I feared they'd take all of the creative control." But once he had a chance to think about the opportunities, Cruikshank started to change his mind. "It hit me one day that a Fred movie could be really cool because the fans would get to see so many of the characters, like Judy, Kevin, Bertha and the mom—the whole Fred world."

In 2010, *Fred: The Movie* debuted on the Nickelodeon cable television network. It drew 7.6 million viewers, making it the year's No 1 cable television movie for kids. *Fred: The Movie* stars Cruikshank as Fred, "iCarly" star Jennette McCurdy as Bertha, wrestler John Cena as Fred's dad, and Siobhan Fallon as Fred's mom. The story opens with Fred feeling devastated because his beloved Judy, played by British pop star Pixie Lott, has moved away. Fred decides to set off on an adventurous journey to Judy's new house. Along the way, he meets many challenges, overcomes some large obstacles, and hatches a plan to get revenge on his arch-rival Kevin, who is also Judy's boyfriend. The movie release was accompanied by the full-length music album *Who's Ready to Party?*, which included some tracks featured in the film. In December 2010 *Fred: The Movie* was released in theaters across the United Kingdom.

Making a movie about Fred allowed Cruikshank to do things he had not been able to do in the video series. "In the movie, you get to see it from a different point of view," he explained. "On YouTube, it's just Fred's point of view, just him and his webcam when he's video blogging. In the movie, you get to see more layers than you get to see in the videos." Another difference is that in the movie, Fred is portrayed as a teenager. "I feel that Fred has always been a 15-year-old—or 14-year-old, or whatever. The thing is, he's still, like, trapped in the mentality of a six-year-old. Obviously, when you watch the videos, I don't look like a six-year-old. I think that he's just trapped in the mentality of a six-year-old." Despite his initial reluctance to take Fred to the big screen, Cruikshank said the movie "turned out better than I ever could have expected."

Cruikshank has earned recognition from the entertainment industry. In 2010, he was named by *Hollywood Reporter* as one of the 50 Most Powerful Players in Digital Media. He was also named by *Variety* as one of the Top

Cruikshank as Fred with Pixie Lott as Judy in a scene from Fred: The Movie.

Ten Comics to Watch. However, not everyone at *Variety* agreed with that assessment. A *Variety* review of *Fred: The Movie* warned that audiences would have reason to be "absolutely horrified" by Cruikshank's "deliberately irritating character," calling his success "inexplicable" and "unfathomable." "I made the movie for the fans," Cruikshank responded. "I didn't make it for the critics. All of my fans really liked it. We tested the movie before we put it out. We had a bunch of test audiences with kids, the core demographic, and it tested amazingly. I think we did the job pretty well."

Future Plans

As a result of his success with Fred Figglehorn, Cruikshank has several new projects planned, including a sequel to *Fred: The Movie*. Nickelodeon has also signed him to star in a new television sitcom called "Marvin, Marvin," about a high school student who has trouble fitting in because he is from another planet. Cruikshank will also star in the upcoming film *Emo Boy*, based on the graphic novel series about a boy who believes he has special EMO "extra-sensitive emotional" powers. And he is also planning to produce more Fred videos, though he admits "I think Fred's almost done. I mean, I've been doing it for four years, and it seems so much longer to me than four years. I think it's time."

"Everything that is happening is really exciting to me," Cruikshank said. "When I first started making videos on YouTube I got a bunch of haters who tried to discourage me by saying to stop making videos. If I would have stopped then none of this would have ever happened. You have to focus on the positive and have fun with it." He is still surprised by all of the opportunities available to him. "I never expected any of this—I lived in Nebraska. It shows that, seriously, anything can happen. Fred Figglehorn? Who knew?"

HOME AND FAMILY

Cruikshank lives in Nebraska with his family, four dogs, two cats, and two cockatiels. He travels frequently to Los Angeles for meetings, filming, and other work. "I think it's awesome living in Nebraska. I like going out to California, but I love coming home and living a totally normal life with my family and friends."

WORKS

"Fred," 2006- (YouTube video series)
It's Hackin' Christmas with Fred, 2009 (CD)
Fred: The Movie, 2010 (movie)
Who's Ready to Party? 2010 (CD)

HONORS AND AWARDS

Choice Web Star (Teen Choice Awards): 2009
50 Most Powerful Players in Digital Media (*Hollywood Reporter*): 2010
Ten Comics to Watch (*Variety*): 2010

FURTHER READING

Periodicals

Girls' Life, Oct./Nov. 2010, p.58
Los Angeles Times, Sep. 16, 2010
New York Times, Dec. 8, 2009
Omaha World Herald, Sep. 18, 2010, p.E1
USA Today, Sep. 17, 2010, p.D9
Washington Post, Sep. 15, 2010, p.A19

Online Articles

http://www.avclub.com
    (The A.V. Club, "Lucas Cruikshank, a.k.a. 'Fred'," Oct. 26, 2010)
http://gigaom.com
    (NewTeeVee, "Fred Speaks to NTV (Squeaky Voice Not Included)," June 25, 2008)

http://www.people.com
   (People, "Five Things to Know About Lucas Cruikshank," Sep. 18, 2010)
http://www.seventeen.com
   (Seventeen, "Everything You Ever Wanted to Know about Lucas Cruikshank (YouTube's Fred!)," Dec. 2, 2009; "Meet Fred Star Lucas Cruikshank," no date)

ADDRESS

Lucas Cruikshank
The Collective
8383 Wilshire Blvd., #1050
Beverly Hills, CA 90211

WORLD WIDE WEB SITE

http://lucascruikshank.org

Jason Derülo 1989-
American Singer and Songwriter
Singer of the No. 1 Hits "Whatcha Say" and "In My Head"

BIRTH

Jason Derülo was born Jason Joel Desrouleaux (pronounced day-ROO-low) on September 21, 1989, in Miramar, Florida. His parents, Joel and Jocelyne Desrouleaux, had immigrated to the United States from the Caribbean nation of Haiti. To support Jason and his older brother and sister, their father worked for the federal government and their mother worked as a bank manager and an immigration officer. Jason Desrouleaux changed the spelling of his last name to "Derülo" when he became a professional performer to make it easier for his fans to pronounce.

YOUTH

Derülo grew up in Broward County, Florida, near Fort Lauderdale and just north of Miami. He was interested in music from a young age, especially after he discovered singer Michael Jackson. "I was a huge Michael Jackson fan growing up," he recalled. "I studied his videos and copied all his moves. I'd also practice singing Usher and Justin Timberlake songs while doing their moves." Even at a young age, Derülo felt a drive to perform. And with a large extended family living in south Florida, there were plenty of opportunities to perform for his family. "Really, my only musical influence—as I was growing up—was school and television," he explained. "Because I didn't have anybody in my household that sang, or did any kind of performing, AT ALL! So for me, it all really came from the inside. I just always had this desire to sing and perform. And with me having tons of cousins—my grandmother had 15 kids—there was always a birthday! And so I'd be singing and dancing at every family function! You know, it was a huge love of mine that I just continued doing for years and years."

> "I just always had this desire to sing and perform," Derülo recalled. "And with me having tons of cousins— my grandmother had 15 kids—there was always a birthday! And so I'd be singing and dancing at every family function!"

Derülo soon wanted a wider audience than just his family, and at age seven he entered his first talent show. At first, he was struck by stage fright. "I remember being backstage and saying, 'I'm not going out there. There are people out there!'" he recalled. "This guy had to pick me up and literally place me on the stage. Then the music came on, and I started singing 'Ben' by Michael Jackson, and I was fine." His family supported his interest in music by enrolling him in a performing arts school, starting in third grade. That was the age he also started writing songs. His first song was a ballad called "Crush on You," which he never shared with the girl that inspired it.

In performing arts school, Derülo studied all kinds of music, from classical and opera to jazz and musical theater. He took a variety of dance classes, including ballet and tap, training he would later use while performing with a professional hip-hop dance company. He spent his free time writing songs; he recorded demos in his mother's car by soundproofing the vehicle and singing into his laptop computer. When he was 12 years old he met Frank Harris, a law student and former basketball player. Derülo had been cut from his junior high school basketball team, so he was practicing on a neighborhood court, and Harris offered to help him improve his game. After having trouble competing with Harris, Derülo told him, "Basketball isn't my thing anyway, I'm a singer." Harris realized the young man wasn't bragging about his musical talents and offered to contact some friends in the New York music industry on his behalf. The contacts helped Derülo sell some of his songs to professionals, and Harris became his manager. For Derülo, it was his first step on the road to becoming an internationally famous performer.

EDUCATION

Derülo attended Dillard School of the Arts, a public high school in Fort Lauderdale, Florida, that was also a performing arts magnet school. (The school is now called Dillard Center for the Arts.) There, he had lead roles in musical productions and also played on the basketball team. After graduating from Dillard in 2005, he moved to New York City to attend the prestigious American Musical and Dramatic Academy (AMDA), a post-secondary school that offers two- and four-year programs. He enrolled in its intensive two-year musical theater program, where he studied dance (including tap), singing, and acting. He graduated from AMDA in 2006 with a certification in musical theater.

CAREER HIGHLIGHTS

Winning the Apollo Theater Competition

After graduating from AMDA, Derülo was offered a part in the Broadway musical *Rent,* the long-running rock musical about struggling artists in New York. It was a prestigious job—*Rent* won both the Pulitzer Prize for drama and the Tony Award for best musical after its 1996 opening—but it would have required a year-long commitment to the role. Derülo decided to chase his dream of becoming a recording artist instead.

The same year Derülo graduated from AMDA, he competed in a talent competition at the famous Apollo Theater in New York's Harlem neighborhood. Amateur Night at the Apollo first debuted in 1934 and was the forerunner to talent competitions like "Star Search" and "American Idol." Contestants could perform any kind of act, but they risked being booed off the stage—audiences at the Apollo have long been known for expressing their

A 2009 portrait of Derülo.

opinions quite forcibly. "Once you play there, you can play anywhere," Derülo recalled of the competition. He participated in the 2006 season, which was televised as "Showtime at the Apollo," and won the overall top prize. He thought he was on his way to success, but "actually, the Apollo didn't really help me out at all, and I was surprised," he remembered. "I was really excited. I thought everything would start happening for me. But it was when I started writing songs for people that the doors opened."

Derülo's manager helped him secure a deal with Rondor Music Publishing, and Derülo started writing songs for other performers. He was still a teenager when Birdman, a rapper from New Orleans, recorded his song "Bossy" in 2007. Derülo also contributed vocals to the track. These efforts led to work writing for rhythm & blues (R&B) singer Cassie and rapper Big Daddy Kane. Derülo also contributed vocals to the 2007 song "My Life," which he co-wrote for Miami rapper Pitbull. Later he wrote songs for Grammy-winning rapper Lil Wayne, chart-topping girl group Danity Kane, and teen rapping sensation Sean Kingston. Although his songwriting was getting him work, he hated giving up his songs to other performers. "It was killing me," he noted. "I had a huge attachment to the songs I was writing, but I had to give them up to make a quick buck. Being in music, I was just hoping something would happen, that someone would notice me."

"I'm not just an urban artist," Derülo stressed. "I want to make music for the world. I want to break musical barriers and not be pigeonholed by the color of my skin to do a certain kind of music."

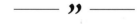

One person who noticed Derülo was producer J.R. Rotem, who had signed Kingston as the first artist to his new Beluga Heights label. Rotem's brother had discovered Derülo through his MySpace page and brought him to Rotem's attention. The producer invited Derülo to come out to Los Angeles to explore his abilities as a songwriter. After hearing him sing in the studio, however, Rotem saw his potential as a performer. Derülo, in turn, felt something click when working with Rotem. "We recorded six songs that night and even though other labels were putting their offers on the table, the music was so compelling that I didn't leave without signing a deal with J.R.," he recalled. When Rotem brought Beluga Heights into a partnership with giant entertainment company Warner Brothers, Derülo was the first artist he planned to promote. The deal introduced Derülo to

Kara DioGuardi, the songwriter and former judge on "American Idol" who was also a Warner Brothers senior vice president in charge of developing talent. With support from her and Rotem, Derülo began creating a great song to introduce himself to the world.

Inspiration for His First Hit Single

Because Derülo was young, he often looked beyond his own experiences for song material. One day his older brother called, upset because his girlfriend had left him. He had cheated on her, but he still loved her and wanted her back. "Because the way he told it to me was so compelling," Derülo said, "I was like, 'If you explain it to HER the way you've just done to ME, maybe she'll give you another chance.'" At the time, Derülo and Rotem were playing around with a sample by British artist Imogen Heap, known for her experimental electronic style. Derülo explained how he came across Heap's music: "I'm the kinda guy that goes into the record store and just picks up any random CD just cause I've never heard of it before. And Imogen Heap is one of those people that I just picked up." Her 2005 song "Hide and Seek" contained a lyric addressed to a cheating lover: "Whatcha say? That you only meant well? Of course you did." Derülo took the sample, combined it with his brother's situation, and came up with the song "Whatcha Say."

"Whatcha Say" was released as a single in summer 2009 and became a huge success. It hit No. 1 on both the *Billboard* Hot 100, which measures radio airplay and sales, and the *Billboard* Pop 100, which measures airplay on mainstream Top 40 stations. The single also reached the Top 10 in England, Canada, Australia, Sweden, Switzerland, Germany, and Japan. When the single finally dropped from the Pop 100 No. 1 after four weeks, it was replaced by Iyaz's "Replay," a song Derülo had co-written for his Beluga Heights label mate. Gradually, he became more comfortable having other performers sing his songs. "It was a little frustrating for me, because these artists got to be the voice while I was behind the scenes, where I always wanted to be the person delivering my lyrics and stuff," he admitted. "It feels really good that I can do that at this stage. I feel really comfortable writing for other people now." He even enjoyed the challenge of matching a song to a performer's personality.

Derülo's success with his first single led to more opportunities. He got an offer to tour with Lady Gaga, who was the biggest new artist of 2009 and the top-selling artist of 2010. He spent the first weeks of 2010 opening for the glamorous and inventive singer. "She's a really great performer and it forced me to step my game up," he noted. "It's just amazing that I'm on

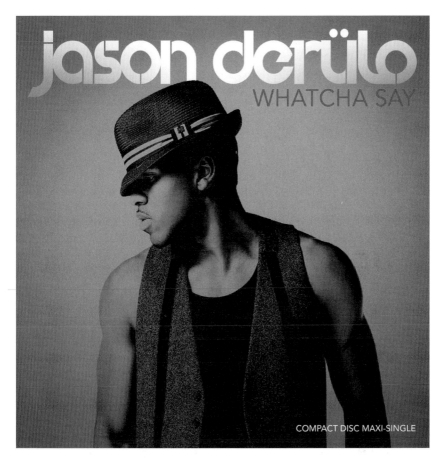

Derülo's first single hit No. 1 on the Billboard charts.

the same show with her." Not long after finishing his tour with Gaga, Derülo released a second single. "In My Head" hit No. 5 on the Hot 100 and followed "Whatcha Say" to the No. 1 spot on the Pop 100 chart. The top placement made Derülo the first male solo artist in the 17-year history of the radio airplay chart to have his first two singles hit No. 1.

In early 2010 Derülo also got a chance to show off his acting skills, appearing in MTV's television movie *Turn the Beat Around.* The movie followed the struggles of a young dancer trying to hit the big time by bringing disco music to a new nightclub. Derülo played a pop star searching for new dancers to perform in his video. "I was really proud of that film because I got the role before I had the musical success," he related. After his single "Whatcha Say" became popular, they changed the role so he was playing

51

himself instead of a character. "It started out I was playing a pop star with a made-up name and now I'm the real pop star!" Throughout the first half of 2010, Derülo got more national exposure with television appearances on "American Idol" and several daytime and late-night talk shows, like "Ellen" and "The Tonight Show."

First Album and First Solo Tour

Derülo released his first album in March 2010, the self-titled *Jason Derülo*. He had waited to release the album, as he explains here. "I wanted people to get to know me as an artist first," he said. "Dropped another single first, and they can see the versatility, because I reinvent myself on each song. You can't really get to know somebody after one song, so I didn't want to drop my album before they were ready for it." Derülo had devoted a lot of effort to the album, working 20-hour days and recording 300 songs in the studio with Rotem before choosing the best nine. "I worked really, really hard on this album to make sure that every single song could stand on its own, and every single song could potentially be a single, and every single song a reinvention, just totally different," he said. Although he could have brought in guest artists for some of the tracks, he decided to establish his own voice and let his music stand on its own.

The album included a wide variety of musical styles. "At one point I was doing straight rock, at another point I was doing Euro dance stuff," Derülo recalled. "I realized I didn't have to choose." The singer noted that although he is African American, "I'm not just an urban artist.... I want to make music for the world. I want to break musical barriers and not be pigeonholed by the color of my skin to do a certain kind of music." The album peaked at No. 11 on the *Billboard* 200 Album chart and stayed on the chart for seven months. According to *Guardian* critic Caroline Sullivan, "He's followed an increasingly well-trodden path to R&B success by first serving an apprenticeship as a songwriter (for Lil Wayne, Diddy, et al.), so he's got the craft of making modern, hyper-slick tunes nailed."

Derülo continued his success on the charts with his third single from the album, "Ridin' Solo," which hit No. 9 on the Hot 100 and stayed on the chart for seven months. A fourth single, the tender ballad "What If," also hit the Top 40 of the pop charts. After opening for the Black Eyed Peas on some of their summer concerts, he set off on his own tour as a headliner. He played dates in Asia, Australia, Europe, and the United States throughout the last half of 2010. "Jason Derülo has got the whole contemporary soul pop package," *Boston Globe* contributor Sarah Rodman said about one tour stop. "He can sing (well enough), he moves beautifully, and he writes

Derülo at the 2010 MTV Video Music Awards.

songs of such breezy joy it's as if they're made of air, smiles, sugar, and electronic handclaps." Derülo finished off 2010 by winning a Teen Choice Award for Choice R&B Album and earning MTV Music Video award nominations for best new artist and best male video, both for the dance-heavy video for "In My Head."

As 2011 began, Derülo promised something different for his second album, which he hoped to release later that year. "I've literally been around the world and back," he said. "I've experienced a lot of ups and downs. I've grown as an artist. There's a totally huge side of my artistry that people have yet to see, so I'm looking forward to the near future." He planned to expand his style by working with other producers as well as Rotem. His method of writing would remain the same, though. "I never write songs down—I feel like the pen dilutes the music," he explained. "I get a concept, go into the [recording] booth and just start singing. I start off with a melody and then figure out the words to match."

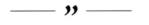

> "I don't feel like I'm competing with other artists," Derülo noted. "I'm just going to try and be the best I can be. And when I get to that level, well, I'll figure out a way to get better."

Although Derülo has had a fantastic start as a singer, he wanted to remind his fans that he is a triple-threat performer, trained in both acting and dance. "While music is very much at the forefront for me now," he said, "in the long-term I can see the acting becoming equally important in my career." He hoped to guest-star on the musical show "Glee," perhaps portraying a character who was a class clown, like he was in high school. Whatever his future brings, he plans to work hard and learn from his peers. "I don't feel like I'm competing with other artists," Derülo noted. "I'm just going to try and be the best I can be. And when I get to that level, well, I'll figure out a way to get better."

HOME AND FAMILY

Although Derülo now makes his home in Los Angeles, he often spends time with his family in the Miami area. "I was one of those kids who couldn't be far from home," he said of his years at school in New York. "I'm still like that." While touring, he travels with his brother and cousin, and tries to fly his mom out for a visit every month.

HOBBIES AND OTHER INTERESTS

Derülo doesn't have much time for hobbies, but he does enjoy using social media like Twitter and Facebook to interact with his fans. He also enjoys movies, especially comedies. He is quick to donate his time and money to charity, a habit he said he learned from his generous mother. As a youth, he grew out his hair for five years and then donated 14 inches of hair to Locks of Love, a charity that makes wigs for cancer patients. He has worked with other cancer charities as well, and has visited children's hospitals while on tour. The singer has also donated money and worked with charities that benefit his family's homeland of Haiti; after the January 2010 Haiti earthquake, he performed at several concerts where the proceeds benefited the victims.

SELECTED CREDITS

Recordings

Jason Derülo, 2010

Television Appearances

"Showtime at the Apollo," 2006
Turn the Beat Around, 2010 (TV movie)

HONORS AND AWARDS

Season Finale Grand Championship ("Showtime at the Apollo"): 2006
Teen Choice Award: 2010, for Choice Music Album-R&B, for *Jason Derülo*

FURTHER READING

Periodicals

AMDA Alumni Spotlight, fall 2010, p. 2
Baltimore Sun, Sep. 30, 2010
Billboard, Oct. 10, 2009, p. 86
Boston Globe, Sep. 30, 2010
Guardian (London), Feb. 26, 2010, p.9
Jet, Jan. 11, 2010, p.22
Miami Herald, Dec. 27, 2009
New York Times, Mar. 6, 2010, p.C1
USA Today, Mar. 15, 2010, p. 3D

Online Articles

http://www.beatweek.com
    (Beatweek Magazine, "Jason Derülo Interview," Mar. 9, 2010)

http://www.billboard.com
  (Billboard, "Jason Derülo Takes Off with 'Whatcha Say' Single," Oct. 6,
  2009; "Jason Derülo Makes History on Pop Songs Chart," Apr. 12, 2010;
  "Jason Derülo Recording 'Dark Material' for Sophomore Album," Sep.
  24, 2010)
http://www.bluesandsoul.com
  (Blues and Soul Magazine, "Jason Derülo: Whatcha Think?" Nov. 30,
  2009)
http://www.cnn.com
  (CNN.com, "Jason Derülo: The Man behind the Hit," Dec. 23, 2009)
http://www.goerie.com
  (Erie [PA] Times-News, "Pop/R&B Star Jason Derülo Performs at Gan-
  non," Apr. 22, 2010)
http://www.mtv.com
  (MTV, "Jason Derülo," Oct. 1, 2010)
http://www.popeater.com
  (Popeater.com, "About to Pop: Jason Derülo," Nov. 12, 2009)
http://www.singersroom.com
  (Singers Room, "Jason Derülo: Perfect Timing," Dec. 22, 2009)

ADDRESS

Jason Derülo
Beluga Heights/Warner Bros. Records Inc.
PO Box 6868
Burbank, CA 91510

WORLD WIDE WEB SITE

www.jasonderulo.com

Angelina Jolie 1975-

American Actor and Humanitarian
Star of the Movies *Girl, Interrupted*; *Lara Croft: Tomb Raider*; *Mr. & Mrs. Smith*; and *Kung Fu Panda*
Goodwill Ambassador for the United Nations High Commissioner for Refugees

BIRTH

Angelina Jolie Voight was born on June 4, 1975, in Los Angeles, California. Her father, Jon Voight, is an Academy Award-winning actor. Her mother, Marcheline Bertrand, was an actor and homemaker. Jolie has one older brother named James Haven Voight. When Jolie was 16 years old, she stopped using her famous father's last name in order to pursue an acting career independent of his reputation. "I dropped my name because it was important that I become known as my own person."

YOUTH AND EDUCATION

Jolie's parents separated before her first birthday and divorced in 1978 when Angelina was about three years old. After the divorce, Jolie's mother took her and her brother to live in Palisades, New York. As a child, Jolie had very little contact with her father.

> *Though Jolie enjoyed acting on make-believe stages as a child, she was not interested in movies at all. "Growing up, I couldn't have cared less about movies. [My brother James] had to drag me to them."*

As a young girl, Jolie liked to play dress up. She loved wearing clothing and costumes that were very feminine, frilly, and sparkly. She created elaborate skits, plays, and theater games with her brother and friends. Her mother made costumes, and her brother would sometimes film her performances with his video camera. Though Jolie enjoyed acting on make-believe stages as a child, she was not interested in movies at all. "Growing up, I couldn't have cared less about movies. [My brother James] had to drag me to them." Despite her lack of interest, when Jolie was about seven years old her father gave her a small role in the 1982 movie *Lookin' to Get Out*, which he co-wrote. She appeared in one brief scene.

In 1986, when Jolie was 11 years old, her mother moved the family to Beverly Hills, California. Her father did not provide much financial support to his children and ex-wife, and the family had to depend only on her mother's income. They lived in small apartments and wore secondhand clothes. Jolie did not fit in very well with her Beverly Hills classmates. She was teased a lot at school because she wore eyeglasses and had braces on her teeth for a while. Classmates also made fun of her for being too skinny and for having big lips. For Jolie, that was a turning point. "At some point, I got closed off, darker."

By the time she was a teenager, Jolie was involved in the Los Angeles punk and grunge music scene. She dyed her hair purple, dressed in scruffy black clothes, and began collecting knives. She was obsessed with death and wanted to become a funeral director. She began experimenting with drugs when she was about 14. "I had a lot of sadness and distrust. I came very close to the end of my life a few times," Jolie later explained. "I think now that if somebody would have taken me at 14 and dropped me in the middle of Asia or Africa, I'd have realized how self-centered I was, and that there was real pain and real death—real things to fight for, so that I wouldn't have been fighting myself so much. I wish, when I was thinking about suicide, I'd have seen how many people are dying each day that have no choice in the matter. I would have appreciated the fact that I had a choice."

Jolie dropped out of public school in 1989 and enrolled in acting classes at the Lee Strasberg Theatre Institute in Beverly Hills. There she studied method acting, an approach that requires actors to draw upon their own personal memories and life experiences to feel the emotions of their characters. Jolie appeared in several productions but left the Strasberg Institute after about a year. She felt that she was too young to have had enough life experience to properly use the method acting approach.

In 1990, Jolie returned to Beverly Hills High School. She completed her coursework early and graduated in 1991, when she was 16 years old. By then, she knew she wanted a career as a movie actor. She moved into her own apartment and began private acting lessons with her father. At that time, Jolie also started modeling with Finesse Model Management. Working as a fashion model gave her more confidence in her appearance and valuable experience being photographed and filmed.

CAREER HIGHLIGHTS

In the early 1990s, Jolie acted in several music videos and five films produced by her brother for his film school classes. She auditioned for and won small roles in several movies and stage plays. Her first major role was in the 1995 crime thriller *Hackers*, starring an ensemble cast of unknown young actors. Jolie played the role of Kate Libby, a young hacker who works with a group of friends to stop an evil genius from releasing a dangerous computer virus. At the same time, the group must hide from Secret Service agents who believe they are responsible for creating the virus. *Hackers* received mixed reviews from movie critics. Most reviewers complained that the plot moved too slowly and the characters were not believable. However, film critic Roger Ebert said that *Hackers* was "well directed, written, and acted" and that Jolie in particular was "convincing and engaging."

Early Success

Jolie's performance in *Hackers* gave her the exposure she needed to win more movie roles. In the late 1990s, she appeared in several theatrical re-

Jolie in stills from three early films:
George Wallace *(top)*, Hackers *(middle)*,
and Girl, Interrupted *(bottom)*.

leases and made-for-television movies. In 1997 she appeared in *George Wallace*, a television drama about the life of former Alabama governor George Wallace. Jolie played Wallace's wife Cornelia in this story set during the battle to end racial segregation in the southern U.S. She won her first Golden Globe award for that performance. In 1998, she appeared in the lead role of the HBO movie *Gia*. This movie told the story of the tragic life and death of 1970s supermodel Gia Carangi. *Variety* praised Jolie's portrayal of Carangi as "a multi-faceted revelation," and her performance garnered a Screen Actors Guild Award and another Golden Globe award.

In 1999, Jolie appeared in *Girl, Interrupted,* a drama about a group of women confined to a mental hospital in the late 1960s. The movie was based on a 1993 memoir by author Susanna Kayson about her own stay in a mental institution and the women she met there. The movie focused on the experiences of Susanna, played by Winona Ryder, the movie's star. Jolie played a rebellious, loud patient named Lisa who befriends Susanna. To the surprise of many critics, she outshone Ryder. The *New York Times* said that Jolie's "ferocious, white-hot performance captures the scary allure of this daredevil and brutal truth-teller," and the *Boston Globe* called her performance "high-voltage." Jolie won her second Screen Actors Guild Award, her third Golden Globe, and an Oscar. She was just 24 years old.

That same year, Jolie appeared in *Pushing Tin*, the story of a group of air traffic controllers that was not successful with critics or at the box office. She followed that with a small role alongside Nicolas Cage in *Gone in 60 Seconds*, a 2000 action drama about a group of car thieves who must steal 50 cars in one night in order to stop a major crime lord from killing one of their own. Many movie critics panned it, with a reviewer for *Variety* calling it "perfectly dreadful in every respect." But the action sequences, special effects, and car chases made the movie a hit with theater audiences.

Lara Croft: Tomb Raider

Jolie's first major starring role was as the title character in the highly anticipated 2001 action film *Lara Croft: Tomb Raider*. The movie was based on *Tomb Raider,* the most successful video game series of the 1990s, which included five games that ultimately sold more than 20 million copies worldwide. At the time Jolie was cast in the movie, the daredevil adventurer Lara Croft was one of the most recognizable video game characters in the world.

To prepare for this physically demanding role, Jolie had to transform herself into an action hero. "I felt like this little geek, this scrawny young actress from L.A.," she said about arriving on the movie set. "I was extremely

Jolie's performance as Lara Croft made her an international superstar.

out of shape. I had not gone to the gym in years. And then through all the training, my body had changed and my mind had changed because I had a totally different focus." She followed a special weight training routine and diet program. She studied kickboxing, learned to race motorbikes and dog sleds, and trained with various weapons. Jolie did most of her own stunts in the movie, including complicated gymnastic moves while hanging from a bungee cord.

Lara Croft: Tomb Raider is the action-packed story of the global search for a legendary artifact called the Triangle of Light. Lara races a group of mercenaries to locate this ancient artifact, which was broken into two pieces and hidden long ago in order to prevent anyone from accessing its great power. If the two pieces are joined together at the precise moment that all the planets in the solar system are in perfect alignment, the holder of the triangle will be able to travel through time. Lara must locate the pieces of the artifact and prevent the mercenaries from using its power to implement their own evil plans. *Lara Croft: Tomb Raider* did not fare well with movie critics. *Variety* called the film "flat and unexciting," while *Entertainment Weekly* said it was a "temple of numb." In spite of such poor reviews, the movie was a huge hit with fans. It became one of Paramount movie studio's highest grossing films, earning $275 million worldwide. And some critics praised Jolie's performance. "Jolie makes a splendid Lara Croft, although to say she does a good job of playing the heroine of a video game is perhaps not the highest compliment," said Roger Ebert of the *Chicago Sun-Times*. "Ever the living fireworks display, Angelina Jolie kicks butt in *Tomb Raider*," Karen S. Schneider wrote in *People*.

For Jolie, the film proved to be a turning point, both professionally and personally. Playing Lara Croft was her first real breakout role and launched her on the road to becoming an international superstar. It was also the first time that a woman had played a major action hero, and the movie's box-office success proved that a female lead could carry an action movie. In addition, it marked a change in her personal life, as she became more aware of and involved in human rights issues.

Working with the United Nations

Filming *Lara Croft: Tomb Raider* required Jolie to travel to many locations around the world, including some remote parts of Cambodia, a country near Vietnam in Southeast Asia. There she first learned about the terrible living conditions of most Cambodian villagers. Thousands of unexploded land mines are still buried in the ground throughout the country, left there during several decades of war in the late 20th century. Unexploded land mines last long after a war is over. Many Cambodian people have been killed or severely injured by stepping on a mine, which is a particular threat for these who live in rural areas. According to the BBC, "Cambodia's chronic mine contamination problem means the threat of death or serious injury is a daily reality for most people here." Jolie was appalled by this and became determined to help the Cambodian people and others in similar situations.

Jolie began to educate herself by reading reports from the United Nations (UN) on global poverty and the harsh living conditions of refugees around the world. "I remember sitting up for two days straight and reading everything obsessively," she stated. Soon after, she approached the UN to find out what she could do to help.

The UN sent Jolie on her first mission, a goodwill trip to the African nation of Sierra Leone. Sierra Leone has been ravaged by civil war for many years, resulting in a large number of refugees who have either fled or been driven from their homes. Jolie was shocked by what she observed on that trip. "I had no idea what a difficult life was. It was as if someone slapped me across the face and said, 'Oh, my God, you silly young woman from California, do you have any idea how difficult the world really is for so many people?' I got out of myself pretty quickly, being in the middle of a civil war."

In 2004 Jolie traveled as a UN goodwill ambassador to Darfur, a region in Sudan that has been the site of an ongoing violent civil war. Here, she is shown talking to children at a displaced persons camp.

Within a few months, Jolie returned to Cambodia on another goodwill trip for the UN. She slept in barracks with the other aid workers, distributed food, washed dishes, and did other jobs as needed. She was most interested in learning all she could by listening and observing. In 2001, Jolie was officially appointed as a goodwill ambassador for the UN High Commissioner for Refugees. In this position, Jolie was able to continue visiting troubled parts of the world as both a fact-finder and an aid worker. That year, she visited Pakistan in South Asia and Tanzania in Africa, and made return trips to Sierra Leone and Cambodia. In 2002, she visited Namibia and Kenya in Africa, Thailand in Southeast Asia, Ecuador in South America, and Serbia in Eastern Europe.

These trips made a huge impact on Jolie. As she met and spoke with refugees in all of these countries, she realized that they "have seen so much, they've felt so much pain—lost more than anyone could bear, and yet they contain joy of life and appreciation for small things we often forget." This realization inspired Jolie to continue doing as much as she could to help people in desperate situations. She also gained a new understanding of her place in the world. "I would never complain again about the stupid things I used to complain about, or be self-destructive, or not realize on a daily basis how lucky I am to have a roof over my head and enough food to eat."

Humanitarian missions and trips around the world were taking up more and more of Jolie's time. Acting began to take a secondary role in her life. She appeared in a few movies, but none did very well with critics or moviegoers. In 2002, she filmed *Lara Croft Tomb Raider: The Cradle of Life*, a sequel to *Lara Croft: Tomb Raider* that was released in 2003. In this movie, Lara is on the hunt for the mythical Pandora's Box, which contains forces of unimaginable evil. Pandora's Box is also sought by a mad scientist with plans to create biological weapons, and Lara must find the box before he does. The movie was scorned by critics but became a hit with fans.

Jolie continued her humanitarian work in 2003, visiting the island nation of Sri Lanka in South Asia, Russia in Northern Europe, Jordan and Egypt in the Middle East, and Tanzania in Africa. During all of her travels, she kept journals of her experiences, thoughts, and impressions. In 2003, Jolie published *Notes from My Travels*, a book based on these journals. In a review of the book, British anthropologist Jane Goodall praised her efforts. "Angelina is living proof of the power we all have—every one of us—to make a difference," Goodall said. "I was deeply moved by her descriptions of individual refugees struggling to live with dignity and hope, and found her personal commitment to be an inspiration." Also in 2003, Jolie received the United Nations Correspondents Association Citizen of the World Award in recognition of her work to bring attention to the challenges faced by the world's refugees.

> —— " ——
>
> *As Jolie spoke with refugees dealing with unthinkable hardships, she gained a new understanding of her place in the world. "I would never complain again about the stupid things I used to complain about, or be self-destructive, or not realize on a daily basis how lucky I am to have a roof over my head and enough food to eat."*
>
> —— " ——

Jolie continued her travels in 2004, when she made her first humanitarian visits within the U.S. She visited three camps in Arizona for immigrants seeking asylum in the U.S. (Asylum is the term used to describe the shelter or protection provided to people who would face risk of death or great harm if they returned to their home country.) Jolie also visited Sudan in Africa, Lebanon in the Middle East, and made a return trip to Thailand.

By this time, Jolie had begun using a large portion of the money she earned from acting to fund her trips. She also began donating millions of dollars to hospitals, schools, children's charities, and refugee organizations. "The reality is I make a ridiculous amount of money to be an actor. And I love being an actor, but I don't need that money," she acknowledged. "Just to have a bunch of money—what do you do with it? What is your life about? But if you know exactly what you're doing with it, and you can see it changing other people's lives, there's a reason for it." For Jolie, the money now had a worthwhile purpose. "I'm able to take the money and see a hospital built or build a well somewhere…. It makes me all that more eager to go to work and be successful because I can do good things."

Appearing in Animated Films

Jolie's next movie project was the 2004 animated feature *Shark Tale*. In this story, a gangster family of sharks suffers a loss when Frankie, next in line to head the crime family, is accidentally killed. Oscar, a lowly nobody fish voiced by Will Smith, takes credit for the murder—even though he didn't kill Frankie—and promptly becomes famous as a "shark slayer." As Oscar takes advantage of his new-found fame, he is pursued by the glamorous gold-digger Lola, voiced by Jolie. Lola is only interested in Oscar because of his celebrity status, and Oscar soon finds that he must make some difficult choices about the direction his life will take. Jolie enjoyed giving Lola a voice, explaining, "One, it's just fun to go to work in your pajamas with no makeup on…. But it's funny to see yourself as a fish. They showed me the pictures of all the different fish, and I saw my fish, and it was so apparent to me very quickly that that was my fish."

Jolie returned to voice acting in 2008 with the role of Tigress in the animated feature film *Kung Fu Panda*. This is the story of a big, bumbling, pot-bellied, black and white panda bear named Po, voiced by Jack Black. Po works in his father's noodle shop but really wants to be a martial arts star. The problem is Po doesn't know anything about martial arts. Through a series of accidents and unexpected events, Po is thought to be the long-awaited Dragon Warrior, the one who will save the town from a menacing, unbeatable enemy. By naming Po as the Dragon Warrior, the ancient sage Oogway passes over other candidates who are much more qualified, including Tigress. Po learns that once he deciphers the Secret of the Dragon Scroll, he will have to battle Tai Lung, the most powerful kung fu master ever

Jolie voiced the character of Tigress in Kung Fu Panda.

known. Even with no knowledge of kung fu, Po must still find a way to defeat Tai Lung. Though movie reviewers gave *Kung Fu Panda* a lukewarm reception, the film was a hit with fans. She will revisit her role as Tigress in *Kung Fu Panda 2*, scheduled for release in 2011. In this sequel, Po joins forces with a new group of kung fu masters to battle an old enemy who now has a deadly new weapon.

Mr. & Mrs. Smith

Jolie's next big role was in the 2005 action-adventure-comedy film *Mr. & Mrs. Smith*. This movie tells the story of Jane Smith, played by Jolie, and her husband John Smith, played by Brad Pitt. On the surface, the Smiths appear to be an average married couple. But each hides a very big secret—they are both professional killers for hire. They have managed to keep their true occupations secret from each other for years, until each receives information about their next job: Mr. and Mrs. Smith have been hired to kill each other. Fast-paced action unfolds as each attempts to carry out these orders, while trying to figure out what the other one is up to. *Mr. & Mrs. Smith* was widely praised by critics and enjoyed by moviegoers. Jolie won three Teen Choice Awards and an MTV Movie Award for her performance.

The chemistry shared onscreen by Jolie and Pitt spilled over into real life, as the couple dealt with tabloid rumors that they had become romantically involved while making the movie. Though both denied having an affair, Pitt soon divorced Jennifer Aniston, his wife of seven years, and moved in with Jolie and her children. Pitt also joined Jolie in her humanitarian work, traveling with her on many official trips and also donating large sums to charitable causes.

Over the following years, Jolie continued to alternate making movies with doing humanitarian work. In 2005, she was honored once again by the UN, which gave her the Global Humanitarian Action Award. In accepting the award, Jolie reaffirmed her commitment to serving those in need. "Second to my children, spending time with refugees and other persons of need around the world has been the greatest gift." In 2006, she took a break from movies in order to focus on her family and her work with the UN. In 2007, Jolie had a part in the epic *Beowulf*, about an ancient warrior who fights against monsters. She also starred in *A Mighty Heart*, based on the memoir of Mariane Pearl, the widow of journalist Daniel Pearl, who was kidnapped and publicly executed by terrorists. As she divided her time between making movies and humanitarian work, Jolie made refugee aid trips to Chad in Africa, Syria in the Middle East, Iraq and Afghanistan in Asia, and made a return trip to Thailand.

Recent Films

In 2008, Jolie appeared in the conspiracy thriller *The Changeling*. This movie is based on the true story of Christine Collins, played by Jolie. Collins is a Los Angeles woman whose nine-year-old son Walter goes missing in 1928. Five months later, the Los Angeles Police Department is under intense pressure to find the boy and close the case. Miraculously, Walter is suddenly found. A staged reunion is planned, with reporters and photographers on hand to capture the moment. During this reunion, Collins realizes that the boy being returned to her is not her son. She confronts the police, trying to point out the mistake. The police respond by committing her to the psychiatric ward of the county hospital, to keep her quiet and avoid exposing what really happened. Jolie's performance in *The Changeling* earned her an Academy Award nomination for Best Actress. Though she did not win the Academy Award that year, by the end of 2008 Jolie was the movie industry's highest-paid female actor. At that time, she was earning an average of $15 million per movie. She continued to use her income to fund her charitable work.

In 2010, Jolie starred in two major films. She played the title character in the spy thriller *Salt*, a role originally written for Tom Cruise and rewritten for Jolie after Cruise declined the role. The story unfolds during a routine interrogation of Russian defector Orlov, who reveals that for many years the Russian government has maintained a network of secret agents within the U.S. These agents were chosen as children and raised their whole lives to become sleeper agents, waiting to trigger a massive attack against the U.S. Orlov then unexpectedly names the CIA agent Evelyn Salt as one of these secret agents. Salt denies this accusation, but then

Jolie with Johnny Depp in a scene from The Tourist.

goes on the run to evade her CIA colleagues. Her motives become even more suspect as the plot develops, and audiences must try to figure out the truth. *Salt* received mixed reviews, with some calling it predictable and other calling it enjoyable fun. "*Salt* knows how to stay one step ahead of you in devious, if jaw-droppingly contrived, ways. The movie is fun," Owen Gleiberman wrote in *Entertainment Weekly*. "The movie builds nuts-and-bolts suspense into the question of who Salt is [and] which side she's on.... *Salt* has enough high-octane reversals to keep you guessing right to the end."

The Tourist focuses on the strange events that happen to a man named Frank, played by Johnny Depp. Frank is an American math teacher, on vacation in Italy to mend his broken heart. Jolie plays Elise, a glamorous mystery woman who deliberately crosses his path. It seems that Elise has chosen Frank to stand in for her former lover, who has been hiding from the police and an angry mobster for the past two years. Elise hopes to use Frank as a decoy to trick the police long enough to retrieve a secret stash of money and escape with it. Elise receives puzzling instructions from her lover in hiding, and as she tries to follow his instructions, a series of plot twists unfolds to keep audiences guessing about how this case of mistaken identity will be resolved. *The Tourist* did not fare well with movie critics, many of whom decried the stilted dialogue, tedious plot, and poor direction, as well as the stars' lack of chemistry and wooden acting. "Stardom can take a terrific story and turn it into a festival of preening earnestness and precious mugging," reviewer Mick LaSalle wrote in the *San Francisco Chronicle.* "Give them a couple of mirrors and have them play the love scenes to their own reflections, and their ardor would be more convincing." Still, Jolie received a Golden Globe nomination for her performance in the film.

Future Plans

Over the course of her career to date, Jolie has appeared in more than 35 movies. In the past nine years, she has made more than 30 goodwill trips on behalf of the UN. Her future plans are to continue dividing her time between acting and humanitarian work, although she is not sure how many more movies she wants to make. "I like acting. It's not the most important thing in my life. Acting helped me as I was growing up. It helped me learn about myself, helped me travel, helped me understand life, express myself, all those wonderful things. So I'm very, very grateful, it's a fun job. It's a luxury.… But I don't think I'll do it much longer."

> "No matter where you live or how old you are, you can decide to change your life. That's amazing," Jolie said. "I believe everyone has a choice: to be a person who does nothing, or a person who does something to make the world better. Maybe you can't fix it. But at least you didn't do nothing.

Jolie has expanded her influence by funding various humanitarian projects through the Jolie-Pitt Foundation, which channels financial donations to charitable organizations around the world. She plans to continue working to raise awareness of causes that are close to her heart, particularly those that benefit the world's refugees. She also works to make progress on international laws governing war crimes. "I am a strong believer that without justice there is no peace. No lasting peace, anyway," she said. "I'm somebody who's very curious about the International Criminal Court.… I think people that do horrible things should be held accountable." She has become a familiar voice in Washington, DC, as she pushes U.S. politicians to take action. "In my early 20s I was fighting with myself. Now I take that punk in me to Washington, and I fight for something important," Jolie explained. "As much as I would love to never have to visit Washington, that's the way to move the ball."

*Jolie with a family on a recent trip to Bosnia, part of her work as a Goodwill
Ambassador for the United Nations High Commissioner for Refugees.*

"No matter where you live or how old you are, you can decide to change
your life. That's amazing," Jolie said. "I believe everyone has a choice: to be
a person who does nothing, or a person who does something to make the
world better. Maybe you can't fix it. But at least you didn't do nothing."

MARRIAGE AND FAMILY

In 1996, Jolie married Jonny Lee Miller, her costar in the movie *Hackers*.
The couple divorced in 2000. Less than one month after the divorce was
final, Jolie married Billy Bob Thornton, her costar in the movie *Pushing Tin*.
The couple divorced in 2003. In 2005 Jolie got involved with Brad Pitt. They
remain unmarried.

In 2002, Jolie adopted a son, Maddox Chivan, from a Cambodian orphanage. Maddox was born on August 5, 2001. In 2005, Jolie adopted a daughter,
Zahara Marley, from an Ethiopian orphanage. Zahara was born on January
8, 2005. Also in 2005, Pitt officially adopted Jolie's children as his own, with
the children taking the last name Jolie-Pitt. On May 27, 2006, Jolie gave
birth to a daughter named Shiloh Nouvel Jolie-Pitt. In 2007, Jolie adopted a
son, Pax Thien Jolie-Pitt, from a Vietnamese orphanage. Pax was born on

November 29, 2003. On July 12, 2008, Jolie gave birth to twins, a son named Knox Leon Jolie-Pitt and a daughter named Vivienne Marcheline Jolie-Pitt.

Jolie travels with her family extensively throughout the world. Jolie and Pitt maintain several homes in different countries.

SELECTED MOVIES

Hackers, 1995
George Wallace, 1997
Gia, 1998
Girl, Interrupted, 1999
Pushing Tin, 1999
Gone in 60 Seconds, 2000
Lara Croft: Tomb Raider, 2001
Lara Croft Tomb Raider: The Cradle of Life, 2002
Shark Tale, 2004
Mr. & Mrs. Smith, 2005
Beowulf, 2007
A Mighty Heart, 2007
Kung Fu Panda, 2008
The Changeling, 2008
Salt, 2010
The Tourist, 2010

HONORS AND AWARDS

Golden Globe Awards: 1998, Best Performance by an Actress in a Supporting Role in a Series, Mini-Series or Motion Picture Made for TV, for *George Wallace*; 1999, Best Performance by an Actress in a Mini-Series or Motion Picture Made for TV, for *Gia*; 2000, Best Performance by an Actress in a Supporting Role in a Motion Picture, for *Girl, Interrupted*
Screen Actors Guild Awards: 1999, Outstanding Performance by a Female Actor in a TV Movie or Mini-Series, for *Gia*; 2000, Outstanding Performance by a Female Actor in a Supporting Role, for *Girl, Interrupted*
Academy Award (Academy of Motion Picture Arts and Sciences): 2000, Best Actress in a Supporting Role, for *Girl, Interrupted*
Citizen of the World Award (United Nations Correspondents' Association): 2003
25 Most Influential Philanthropists in the World (*Worth* magazine): 2003
Global Humanitarian Action Award (United Nations): 2005
Teen Choice Awards: 2005 (3 awards), Choice Movie Actress: Action Adventure/Thriller, Choice Movie Liar, Choice Movie Rumble (with Brad Pitt), for *Mr. & Mrs. Smith*

People's Choice Awards: 2005, Favorite Female Action Movie Star; 2009, Favorite Female Action Star

MTV Movie Award: 2006, Best Fight, for *Mr. & Mrs. Smith* (with Brad Pitt)

FURTHER READING

Books

Schuman, Michael A. *Angelina Jolie: Celebrity with Heart*, 2011

Periodicals

Biography, Oct. 2003, p.42
Christian Science Monitor, Sep. 8, 2010
Current Biography Yearbook, 2000
Entertainment Weekly, June 20, 2008
New York Times, Oct. 19, 2008; Nov. 21, 2008
Newsweek, Mar. 19, 2007
People, May 8, 2002, p.67; Sep. 5, 2005; Aug. 2, 2010
Time, Apr. 30, 2006; Apr. 30, 2009
Vanity Fair, Aug. 2010

Online Articles

http://www.allmovie.com/artist/angelina-jolie-36009/bio
    (AllMovie, "Angelina Jolie Biography," no date)
http://www.nationalgeographic.com
    (National Geographic, "Angelina Jolie on Her UN Refugee Role," June 18, 2003)
http://www.topics.nytimes.com
    (New York Times, "Angelina Jolie," multiple articles, various dates)
http://www.newsweek.com/topics.html
    (Newsweek, "The Secret World of Angelina Jolie: The One Part of Her Life We Don't Obsess Over," July 13, 2010)
http://www.people.com/people/angelina_jolie/biography
    (People, "Angelina Jolie," no date)

ADDRESS

Angelina Jolie
Special Artists Agency
9465 Wilshire Blvd., Ste. 470
Beverly Hills, CA 90212

WORLD WIDE WEB SITES

http://www.un.org/works/goingon/refugees/angelina_story.html
http://www.unhcr.org/pages/49c3646c56.html

Monica Lozano 1956-
American Newspaper Publisher
Chief Executive Officer of *La Opinión*, the Largest
Spanish-Language Daily Newspaper in the U.S., and
ImpreMedia, the Largest Spanish-Language News
Company in the U.S.

BIRTH

Monica Cecilia Lozano was born on July 21, 1956, in Los Angeles, California. Her mother, Marta Navarro Lozano, was a
homemaker. Her father, Ignacio E. Lozano Jr., was the publisher of *La Opinión*, a Spanish-language newspaper. *La*

Opinión was founded in 1926 by his father (Lozano's grandfather), Ignacio E. Lozano Sr. Monica Lozano is the third of four children. She has an older sister, Leticia; an older brother, José; and a younger brother, Francisco.

YOUTH

Lozano grew up in Newport Beach, California. All of her grandparents came to the U.S. from Mexico, and her parents were the first generation born in the U.S. They emphasized the importance of the family's Mexican heritage and made sure that Lozano and her brothers and sister learned about Mexican culture. "We were always taught to really respect and enjoy and value our cultural background and never to forget," she explained. "We weren't allowed to speak English at home. We just literally were not allowed to speak English at home…. Most parents at that time wanted their kids to succeed by not speaking Spanish. My parents wanted us to learn English, but were adamant that we not forget Spanish and where we came from and our roots and all of that. It was really important to them."

> "We were always taught to really respect and enjoy and value our cultural background and never to forget," Lozano explained. "Most parents at that time wanted their kids to succeed by not speaking Spanish. My parents wanted us to learn English, but were adamant that we not forget Spanish and where we came from and our roots and all of that. It was really important to them."

As a child, Lozano learned more about Mexican culture each summer when she visited her extended family in Mexico City. "We were sent to Mexico every year," she recalled. "We would spend our summers in Mexico with my grandmother and all of our cousins. We were the only ones that lived here in the States, so it was really important to maintain the family together." Lozano enjoyed spending time in Mexico. "I liked it much more than I liked it up here," she reminisced. "I had a lot of friends and we had a great life. There's something missing here in the U.S. that you get in a place like Mexico, where family really means family, and extended family really is extended family. You interact as part of a larger group. Here everything is so individualized, that if you're going to succeed, you do it on your own, and you advance on your own. People are much more competitive. I just don't think I ever really liked it as much as I like the other."

A 1940 photo of a Los Angeles couple reading the newspaper founded by Lozano's grandfather, La Opinión, which became the largest Spanish-language daily newspaper in the U.S.

As she got older, Lozano began to realize that she lived in two different worlds—one with her parents in the U.S. and one with her extended family in Mexico. She began to struggle with her identity as she looked for a place to fit in. "You go through periods where you wonder who you really are," she mused. "You go to Mexico and you know you're not Mexican.... You come here and you think, well, this isn't quite right either. It's a phenomenon that I think happens to a lot of Chicano kids that are second or third generation, where you have a real desire to maintain your cultural heritage, but it's not quite one thing or the other."

Lozano also began to learn about Mexico's political environment at a very young age. Her grandfather, Ignacio E. Lozano Sr., had died before she was born, but his story was an important part of the family history. "My grandfather was a journalist, a famous, well-respected, well-known writer from Northern Mexico, who also left during the [Mexican] revolution, mostly because he was writing things against the government and was more sympathetic to the need for change in Mexico." The Mexican Revolution began in 1910, with violent civil war and political unrest that continued for many years. The worst of the revolution ended in 1920, although occasional fighting continued until 1929. During this time, those who spoke out against the Mexican government were forced either to leave the country or risk being jailed or killed for their opinions. Many Mexican citizens fled to the U.S. during these years.

After arriving in San Antonio, Texas, Ignacio E. Lozano Sr. created *El Diario La Prensa* in 1913. This was the first of the Spanish-language newspapers that would become his family's business for generations to come. His goal was to be the voice of the Mexican immigrant community in the U.S. In 1926, he moved to Los Angeles and founded the newspaper *La Opinión*. By this time, the Mexican government had banned him from returning to Mexico. "He wasn't allowed to go back to Mexico because of his political writings," Monica Lozano explained. "It wasn't that he was publishing in Mexico stuff they didn't want; they didn't like what he was publishing up here in the United States. He found that it was the only place where he could actually say what he needed to say."

For Monica Lozano, her grandfather's legacy meant that she grew up surrounded by family members and others who were passionate about Mexican culture, Mexico's future, and keeping Mexican immigrants informed about important issues in the U.S. and in Mexico that affected their lives. Her father, older brother, and older sister all worked at *La Opinión*. Her father was also active in U.S. politics, and served as the U.S. ambassador to El Salvador for one year. During that year, Lozano lived in El Salvador with her parents and her younger brother.

EDUCATION

For her first two years of high school, Lozano attended Marywood, a Catholic girls' school in the city of Orange, California. For her third and fourth years of high school, she attended Santa Catalina School, a Catholic girls' boarding school in Monterey, California. She graduated from high school in 1974.

After high school, Lozano enrolled in the University of Oregon. She was not interested in joining the family newspaper business at that time. Instead, she wanted to pursue a career in social work or education. At the University of Oregon, she studied sociology and political science. She also worked at the Women's Press newspaper. Lozano left the university in 1976 without graduating.

After leaving college, Lozano and a friend traveled extensively throughout Latin America. "The two of us literally started in northern Mexico and made it all the way down to the very tip of South America. When I came back from that trip, I moved to San Francisco and never went back to the university, unfortunately. I would say unfortunately because I think it was a mistake not to have at some point gone back."

While Lozano never returned to the University of Oregon or completed her bachelor's degree, she did enroll in classes at San Francisco City College, a two-year community college, and earned a degree in printing technology in 1981.

CAREER HIGHLIGHTS

Over the course of her career, Lozano has become known as one of the most influential women in U.S. journalism. After working for many years at *La Opinión,* she eventually became the head of the ImpreMedia publishing company, which includes *La Opinión* as well as many other Spanish-language and Spanish-English publications and web sites. Though she inherited a successful, established publishing company when she took over leadership of ImpreMedia, Lozano herself is credited with expanding the family business by creating new publications and web sites. She has often commented that "you can't separate my success from my family," but her success was not automatically guaranteed. Her achievements came only as a result of her own hard work, both at ImpreMedia and during the earlier years she spent deciding whether she wanted to work in the family business at all.

"You go through periods where you wonder who you really are," Lozano mused. "You go to Mexico and you know you're not Mexican.… You come here and you think, well, this isn't quite right either. It's a phenomenon that I think happens to a lot of Chicano kids that are second or third generation, where you have a real desire to maintain your cultural heritage, but it's not quite one thing or the other."

Starting Out

Lozano grew up knowing that newspapers were her family's business. Her grandfather, Ignacio E. Lozano Sr., founded the newspapers; her father, Ignacio E. Lozano Jr., ran them after her grandfather's death; her brother, José Lozano, took over after her father retired; and her sister, Leticia Lozano, worked there as well. The whole family was deeply committed to continuing the work begun by Ignacio E. Lozano Sr. Monica Lozano knew that the newspapers were important, but she wasn't sure that the family business was the right career for her. "I liked *La Opinión* and I liked the idea of what *La Opinión* was doing, but I just wasn't quite convinced that this was going to be my life. I didn't want to follow in anybody's footsteps."

In 1977, after leaving college, Lozano decided to move to San Francisco, though she didn't know anyone there. She got a job at a large printing company and learned to operate a printing press. She also worked for various community newspapers. During this time, she realized that she wanted to help her community. In order to do that, she would need to use all of her skills including her knowledge of newspapers. Lozano became more interested in the newspaper publishing business and decided to learn everything she could about running a paper, including taking classes in printing technology at San Francisco City College.

Although she had set out to make her own way in the world, Lozano ended up back where she started—in the newspaper business. "I guess there is such a thing as having ink in your veins," she observed. In 1985, she moved back to Los Angeles and began working for *La Opinión*.

Working at *La Opinión*

In 1985, Lozano joined the staff of *La Opinión* as a managing editor. During this time, it was still unusual for women to work as journalists. And it was even more unusual for a woman to be in a management position. "I couldn't have done it without my family," she acknowledged. "Literally, I wouldn't be here without the support and the confidence of my family." Lozano had no real experience working for a large daily newspaper but explained that "they really opened the doors and asked me to come in, knowing full well that I didn't have sort of a traditional background and experience that you would find in most managing editors."

In addition to learning the responsibilities of her new job, Lozano also had to learn how to get along in a work environment that was not always friendly to women. In describing one of her early experiences at the newspaper, "I came in not just as the daughter of the owner, but one of the first women in the newsroom," she recalled. "And absolutely, those were the days when, you know, men had pictures of women all over their cubicles … it was just, you know, an entirely different atmosphere and attitude. And the women in the newsroom, when I came in—because I came in, in the position as managing editor—the women in the newsroom immediately asked for a meeting … and lo and behold, they felt harassed and uncomfortable in that environment. But it wasn't until there was a woman in the leadership position that they felt that they actually had an outlet where

Lozano in the newsroom of La Opinion, celebrating with staff members after announcing that the newspaper had won a major journalism award.

their voice not only would be heard, but we actually could do something about changing the culture in that newsroom.... One of the first things that I did was issue memos saying that there will not be any more photographs and there will not be any more whistling.... I mean, really having to say some of the most basic things about how people should treat each other in a work environment."

Lozano's other duties as managing editor included full responsibility for all of the newspaper's special supplements and public service work. She immediately began working on creating newspaper inserts that focused on topics of particular importance or interest to readers. Her first project of this kind focused on the Immigration Reform and Control Act, a major immigration law that passed in 1986. "*La Opinión* knew that it had to do an extraordinary job in informing the community about it. It was a possibility for millions of people to become legalized. They had opened the door and said, 'If you're illegal right now, you've got a couple of years to become legal, to come out of the shadows.' So we did a lot of work on this particular law. We ended up winning awards."

Another of Lozano's big projects in 1986 was the publication of a newspaper insert that focused on the growing threat of the AIDS virus within the

Hispanic community. In 1988, this special publication received an advocacy award from the Hispanic Coalition of AIDS as a life-saving, educational contribution to the community. The AIDS insert also received an award from the Inter-American Press Association.

Moving Up the Corporate Ladder

Lozano was named associate publisher of *La Opinión* in 1990. In this position, she continued to create new publications that contributed to the growth of the newspaper's circulation. She expanded the paper's focus beyond the Mexican immigrant community, to include the more diverse community of native speakers of Spanish from other parts of the world. Lozano also formed partnerships with other organizations in order to better inform the community about health, immigration, education, and other important issues. Under her leadership, *La Opinión* grew to become the largest and most influential Spanish-language publication in the U.S.

In the following years, Lozano continued to move up the corporate ladder. In 2000 she was named president and chief operating officer of *La Opinión* as well as vice president of its parent company, Lozano Communications. In 2004 she became publisher and chief executive officer of *La Opinión*, the top position at the paper.

Also in 2004, ImpreMedia was formed as the parent company of a range of publications, including *El Diario La Prensa*, the oldest Spanish-language daily newspaper in the U.S., founded in 1913 by Lozano's grandfather; and *La Opinión*, the largest Spanish-language daily newspaper in the U.S., founded in 1926 also by Lozano's grandfather. The goal of the new company was to create a national group of Latino media. ImpreMedia provides news and information online and in print format, with daily and weekly newspapers, monthly magazines, and web sites. In addition to *La Opinión* and *El Diario La Prensa*, national publications include the Spanish-language entertainment weekly *La Vibra* and the Spanish-English monthly magazine *Vista*. ImpreMedia also publishes local Spanish-language newspapers including *El Mensajero* in San Francisco, *La Prensa* in central Florida, and *La Raza* in Chicago. The web site Impre.com has grown to be one of the top Spanish-language news sites in the U.S.

When ImpreMedia was created in 2004, Lozano was named senior vice president, overseeing the company's publishing group. In 2010, she became the company's chief executive officer. In that position she now oversees a collection of 27 Spanish-language and Spanish-English newspapers, magazines, and web sites.

Lozano in 2004, at a major moment in her career: her ascension to senior vice president of the new company ImpreMedia and simultaneously to publisher and CEO of La Opinión.

In addition to running a large publishing company, Lozano has served on the board of directors for major U.S. corporations, including Bank of America and the Walt Disney Company. She has also served on the board of directors for non-profit groups, including the California Health Care Foundation, the National Council of La Raza, and the Los Angeles County Museum of Art. She has received honorary degrees from several universities as well as a number of prestigious awards from national media, business, and community groups. In 2009, Lozano was named as a member of President Barack Obama's Economic Recovery Advisory Board, a group of business leaders who help the President decide how best to respond to the U.S. economic crisis.

Changing Perceptions

One of Lozano's lifelong goals has been to help people understand the importance and value of Spanish-language publications for readers in the U.S. She acknowledges that many people believe Spanish-language newspapers and magazines encourage immigrants to remain isolated and outside of American culture. But Lozano believes that is simply not true. "The way that we approach our content, is that we, in fact, are a tool for integration.... So, actually, the newspaper is used not as a way of keeping kids monolingual, but a way of teaching literacy that then allows them to transfer over to English. So it's really a tool towards learning English, and most people I don't think understand that."

———— " ————

"I carry on a tradition that was established by my grandfather," Lozano said. "That mission was to serve the community, which, in that case, was primarily an immigrant population, primarily from Mexico, that needed a source of information about their issues and reflected their reality. Our community today is much more diverse and our scope of influence is much broader, but the core value stays intact."

———— " ————

Lozano feels strongly about the importance of educating readers, especially those who primarily speak Spanish. "As a group, we can have power if we are informed and educated.... I really believe in what I am doing," she explained. "If we were not to exist, you would have millions of people in L.A. who are uninformed and unable to participate. And which is worse? I think it's better for us to exist and to allow people, one, to continue their education through reading newspapers like ours, to be informed, to be able to make decisions, to participate in decision-making processes. We don't advocate staying in the Spanish language completely. We understand that it's important if you're going to be in this country and you're going to succeed and you're going to thrive and survive, you have to speak English, and we say that directly."

Lozano is determined to change the way that Spanish-speaking immigrants are viewed by others. "The worst of it is to hear people say, 'Hispanics don't read.' It's a fallacy. It's absolutely false. I don't know where that came from ... because you can go into any Latin American country and newspapers are so prevalent. I mean, in Mexico City there's over 40 daily newspapers. Everybody reads." Lozano explained that this particular misconception is "one of the reasons why we've made the decision that we have to go bilingual. So for example, all of our editorials are published bilingually because if we have a statement, we want to make sure that it reaches the broadest audience possible."

A Family Legacy

Lozano may not have known right away that the newspaper business would become her life's work, but she is now committed to carrying on the family tradition. "I really love what I'm doing and think I'm good at it and

Lozano working at the White House on the Economic Recovery Advisory Board, alongside (from left) Mark T. Gallogly, Paul Volcker, President Barack Obama, and John Doerr.

think that the paper is doing something that's really valuable," Lozano said. "I know I carry on a tradition that was established by my grandfather.... That mission was to serve the community, which, in that case, was primarily an immigrant population, primarily from Mexico, that needed a source of information about their issues and reflected their reality. Our community today is much more diverse and our scope of influence is much broader, but the core value stays intact."

Lozano's success has come from a combination of unique opportunities and her own dedication to community education and service. "I think I was very fortunate that the opportunity was available to me; clearly something like this is available to only a handful of people. But the fact that I've taken such advantage of it speaks more to me as an individual than the fact that it's just there," Lozano said. "If you are going to do it, you should be prepared to go all the way.

"I always say, one, you know, follow your passion and do what it is that you are most compelled to do, because life is too short to not do things that you absolutely love doing. And the other thing is around both perseverance and also determination.... You don't start at the top. You work your way up. And, you know, constantly just demanding more of yourself, making sure that you're working at the very highest level, and making sure that your reputation is intact as you move along the path of life. Because at the end of the day, that's what you carry with you and that's what people will remember about you. So just make sure, along the way, that you're working hard. When people turn around and say, you know, that woman is really good; I can depend on her—that's what you want them to say about you. You know, strong values: highly ethical, smart decision-making, you know, philosophy—that's what's important."

MARRIAGE AND FAMILY

Lozano married Marcelo Centanino in 1986. The couple had two children, Santiago, born in 1987, and Gabriela, born in 1989. The marriage ended in divorce. Lozano later married her second husband, David Ayala, a political scientist. They live in Los Angeles.

HONORS AND AWARDS

100 Most Influential Hispanic Women (*Hispanic Business*): 1987, 1992
Central American Refugee Center Award: 1988, for contribution to immigrant rights
Outstanding Woman of the Year Award (Mexican American Opportunities Foundation): 1989
National Organization for Women Legal Defense and Education Fund Award (National Organization for Women): 1992
Distinction in Media Excellence Award (March of Dimes): 1992, for special publication on pre-natal care
Hubert H. Humphrey Civil Rights Award (Leadership Conference on Civil Rights): 2006
Marketing y Medios Print Media All-Star of the Year (*Adweek*): 2007
Medallion of Excellence for Leadership and Community Service (Congressional Hispanic Caucus Institute): 2007
PODER-BCG Business Awards (*PODER* magazine and the Boston Consulting Group): 2008, for Excellence in Media
Best Latinos in Business (*Hispanic Magazine*): 2009

FURTHER READING

Books

Ruíz Vicki, and Virginia Sánchez Korrol. *Latinas in the United States: A Historical Encyclopedia,* Vol. 1, 2006

Periodicals

Hispanic Business, Apr. 2004, p.44
Los Angeles Times, May 26, 2010

Online Articles

http://findarticles.com/p/articles/mi_m0PCH/is_1_6/ai_n13661865/
   (B Net, CBS Business Network, "Monica Lozano," Feb-Mar. 2005)
http://www.npr.org
   (NPR.org, "Latina Publishing Magnate Shares Wisdom from the Trade,"
   July 28, 2010)
http://www.wpcf.org/oralhistory/loz.html
   (Washington Press Club Foundation, "Interviews with Monica Lozano,"
   1993-1994)

ADDRESS

Monica Lozano
ImpreMedia
700 South Flower Street
Los Angeles, CA 90017

WORLD WIDE WEB SITE

http://www.impremedia.com

Jane Lubchenco 1947-
American Marine Ecologist and Environmental
Scientist
First Woman to Serve as Administrator of the U.S.
National Oceanic and Atmospheric Administration
(NOAA)

BIRTH

Jane Lubchenco (pronounced loob-CHEN-ko) was born on
December 4, 1947, in Denver, Colorado. Both of her parents
were doctors: her father was a surgeon, and her mother was a
pediatrician. Lubchenco has five younger sisters.

YOUTH

As a child growing up in Denver, Lubchenco enjoyed being outdoors. Family vacations were often spent camping and hiking in the Rocky Mountains. Lubchenco developed an early love of nature, particularly any opportunity to be in the water. She remembers sharing this enthusiasm with her sisters. "My five sisters and I were part fish," she recalled. "We'd seek water anywhere—lakes and rivers in Colorado, the ocean on family trips to Southern California. I remember my first ocean swim, the saltiness of it." Fishing was another one of her favorite pastimes. "I have fond memories of trout fishing with my father in Colorado mountain lakes and streams and, as a high school student, going salmon fishing with him on charter boats in Oregon and Washington."

> "As a Colorado native, I was astounded to discover a wealth of life in oceans. It was a world filled with incredible diversity of forms and functions, from sea stars to lobsters to exotic small creatures.... I had never really appreciated until that summer just the immense diversity and the incredible beauty and the exotic nature of all the different species in the oceans."

EDUCATION

Lubchenco's interest in nature and the environment led her to study biology at Colorado College. As part of her coursework, she participated in a summer program at the Marine Biological Laboratory in Woods Hole, Massachusetts. The Marine Biological Lab is an internationally known scientific research facility located just off the Atlantic Ocean on the southwestern tip of Cape Cod.

Lubchenco had visited the ocean before, but working at the Marine Biological Lab was her first opportunity to study ocean ecology. (Ecology is a branch of biology that focuses on studying communities of plants and animals and their relationship to their surroundings.) "As a Colorado native, I was astounded to discover a wealth of life in oceans. It was a world filled with incredible diversity of forms and functions, from sea stars to lobsters to exotic small creatures, many of whose daily rhythms were profoundly linked to the far away moon and its influence on the earth's tides." The experience made a great impact on Lubchenco. She explained, "I had never really appreciated until that summer just the immense diversity and the incredible beauty and the exotic nature of all the different species in the oceans."

Lubchenco earned a bachelor's degree in biology from Colorado College in 1969. She earned a master's degree in zoology from the University of Washington in 1971. (Zoology is a branch of biology that focuses on studying the unique characteristics of animals.) In 1975, Lubchenco completed her PhD (doctorate) in ecology at Harvard University. Her doctoral studies focused on the ecology of plants and animals that live in rocky coastal waters.

CAREER HIGHLIGHTS

Over the course of her long career, Lubchenco has become known for her deep understanding of ocean ecology. She is recognized as an expert in the relationship between oceans and climate change and the connection between the environment and human health and welfare. Her work is widely seen as both groundbreaking and extremely useful in furthering scientific understanding of oceans and marine life. She has traveled the world studying marine ecology in different areas, including the Arctic regions of Greenland and Alaska as well as the tropics of Central America. She has also studied sea life in the Mediterranean, Europe, China, New Zealand, coastal areas of North America, and many other places. She uses the results of her scientific research to educate people about the current conditions of the world's waterways and to make predictions about the future of oceans and sea life. Lubchenco is also known for her interest in creating practical solutions to problems like pollution and global warming. The Natural Resources Defense Council, an environmental protection group, called her "one of the best-known American voices for marine conservation."

Early in her career, Lubchenco balanced a number of different teaching and research positions. After earning her PhD in 1975, she became an assistant professor at Harvard. In 1978, she moved across the country to begin teaching marine biology at Oregon State University. Also in 1978, Lubchenco began working as a research associate with the Smithsonian Institution in Washington, DC, and as a science advisor for the Ocean Trust Foundation. During this time, her research focused primarily on evolutionary ecology (studying how plants and animals interact with the environment over time).

Understanding Climate Change

Through her research and work around the world, Lubchenco was able to see firsthand the damaging effects of human actions on oceans and marine life. She focused on evolutionary ecology, which compares current and previous environmental conditions and looks for differences between the

Lubchenco, a marine biologist, is shown working in the field.

past and present. By studying environmental changes over time, Lubchenco was one of the first scientists to show evidence that climate change was occurring. She observed and documented the significant environmental damage being done by global warming and pollution. Her studies exposed clear examples of the many ways in which humans have unintentionally caused harm to the environment.

As a result of her findings, Lubchenco realized that people needed to become better stewards of the earth's natural resources. Although she was publishing her studies within the scientific community, she wanted to bring her findings to a larger audience. She knew that further environmental damage could be prevented only through the involvement of government, industry, and the general public. Lubchenco set out to find ways to bring scientific information to the public in forms that would be easy for the average person to understand.

Lubchenco strongly believed that scientists have a responsibility to educate the public about research on important issues. "Science is more than just fascinating knowledge, it is also useful knowledge," she explained. "I believe passionately that science

————— **"** —————

"Most Americans still believe that the oceans are so vast and bountiful that there is very little that we can do that would truly change them," Lubchenco commented. "The reality is that we are not just using oceans—we are using them up. If we truly want to be able to use them tomorrow, we have to do a better job of protecting them today."*

————— **"** —————

should inform our decisions." She saw a gap between the scientific community and the rest of the world, and she wanted to help bridge that gap. Lubchenco realized that scientific researchers were often unprepared to communicate well with non-scientists. To help scientists become better communicators, she founded the Leopold Leadership Program in 1998.

The Leopold Leadership Program was designed to help environmental scientists bring their work to people outside the scientific and academic communities. Lubchenco's goal was to train researchers to talk to government leaders and the media, in the hope that science could inform public policy decisions and law-making. As she explained, "I am not suggesting that scientists should dictate what individuals or societies should do or not do. Rather, I emphasize that one of the most important roles of science is to inform, to provide information, so that decision-makers can take that information into consideration and understand the full ramifications of a course of action."

Teaching public communication skills to scientific researchers was a new idea at that time, and the Leopold Leadership Program was the first organization of its kind. "When we started the program, we were not at all sure that scientists, and the best scientists, would even apply to the program much less to be willing to invest two very intense weeks in learning new skills," Lubchenco recalled. "Much to our delight, and more importantly to the benefit of the nation, we have been overwhelmed by applications from the most outstanding scientists."

The Leopold Leadership Program has been successful in teaching scientists how to explain their work in ways that are both relevant and easy to understand. The program has been especially successful for topics related to global warming and climate change. Lubchenco sees these issues as particularly difficult for non-scientists to absorb. "Assessment of climate change is a good example of the problem that decision-makers face," she observed. "One hears conflicting opinions: on the one hand, 'global warming is happening,' on the other hand someone else says, 'oh no, that's not true.' It's very difficult for most folks to sort through all the conflicting opinions and complex evidence. In its zeal to be 'balanced,' the press often presents 'both sides' with equal credibility, despite the fact that the overwhelming majority of experts agree and are on one 'side.'"

In 2002, Lubchenco was honored for her work with the Leopold Leadership Program. She received the prestigious Heinz Award for the Environment. This award recognized her as one of the most respected and recognized ecologists in the country and praised her efforts to help scientists communicate more effectively. In presenting the award to Lubchenco, Heinz Family Philanthropies said, "She has shown that, while scientists should be excellent, pure and dispassionate, scientists should not sacrifice their right—and must not ignore their responsibility—to communicate their knowledge about how the earth is changing or to say what they believe will be the likely consequence of different policy options."

Moving into Government

By the mid-2000s, Lubchenco's reputation as an environmental expert was firmly in place, acknowledged by other scholars, academic institutions, and governmental agencies. Her experience had grown to include visiting professorships at universities in Chile, China, and New Zealand. She had become a member of the National Academy of Sciences, the American Philosophical Society, the American Academy of Arts and Sciences, the Royal So-

Lubchenco in a briefing for President Barack Obama in the situation room of the White House. Seated at the table (from left to right): Homeland Security secretary Janet Napolitano, National Incident commander admiral Thad Allen, Environmental Protection Agency administrator Lisa P. Jackson, U.S. Coast Guard rear admiral Peter Neffenger, press secretary Robert Gibbs, interior secretary Ken Salazar, NOAA administrator Jane Lubchenco, energy secretary Steven Chu, and chief of staff Rahm Emanuel.

ciety, and the Academy of Sciences for the Developing World, Europe, and Chile. She was a member of the board of directors for the National Science Board, the National Science Foundation, the Joint Oceans Commission Initiative, the Aspen Institute Arctic Commission, and the Council of Advisors for Google Ocean. She headed the Partnership for Interdisciplinary Studies of Coastal Oceans and was a scientific advisor to the U.S. Congress and Presidents George H.W. Bush, Bill Clinton, and George W. Bush. Lubchenco had become one of the most highly respected ecologists in the world.

Lubchenco's successful scientific career prompted President Barack Obama to nominate her for the position of administrator of the U.S. National Oceanic and Atmospheric Administration (NOAA) and U.S. under secretary of commerce for Oceans and Atmosphere. Congress confirmed her nomination in 2009, making Lubchenco the first woman to serve in this role.

The NOAA's area of responsibility stretches from the ocean floor, to the upper reaches of the earth's atmosphere, and beyond to the surface of the sun. Its mission is to understand and predict changes in the earth's environment and to conserve and manage U.S. coastal and marine resources. The NOAA protects, maintains, and restores the sustainability of U.S. oceans and the Great Lakes. The NOAA is also the nation's primary source of information and research on oceans and the atmosphere, and it works to increase scientific understanding of climate change. The National Weather Service is part of the NOAA and operates the nation's weather observation, forecasting, and severe weather early warning systems.

Lubchenco sees her new position as an extension of the work she started with the Leopold Leadership Program. "Being in this job has only reinforced the importance of communicating scientific information in a way that is understandable and relevant to the decisions being made, with concrete examples, and in as unequivocal a fashion as possible, while still remaining true to the nuances that are important," she remarked. "And I think all too many scientists assume that everybody knows what they know, and especially members of Congress, and members of the administration. And so it's critically important that more scientists become bilingual—able to speak the language of science, but also able to speak the language of lay people when talking to non-scientists."

In pursuit of her goal to make more environmental information available to the public, one of Lubchenco's first acts as the head of the NOAA was to create the Climate Service. She described the Climate Service as a source of "trusted, timely, and accessible" climate information. "We are envisioning it as analogous to the National Weather Service," she said. "I believe it's an idea whose time has come." The NOAA has enough information to make climate forecasts in the same way that the National Weather Service provides weather forecasts, according to Lubchenco. However, the Climate Service would be able to provide forecasts for a much longer future time frame. For example, "If you're building a wind farm, you would want to know not just where the winds have been good for the past 100 years, but where they're likely to be good the next 100 years," she explained. "So there are a number of new ways that climate is affecting our lives that if we had some reasonable forecasts for 20- to 30-year horizons, we could be doing a much better job of making decisions about land use, about water management, about crops, about a whole suite of different things."

Ocean "Dead Zones"

In addition to working on climate change, Lubchenco has also focused her work at the NOAA on what she calls the "equally evil" problem of ocean acidification. Ocean acidification describes the result of excessive carbon

NOAA was deeply involved in assessing the damage to natural resources after the 2010 BP oil spill in the Gulf of Mexico. Here, Lubchenco is shown on a survey off the coast of Mississippi taking samples of sea life.

dioxide in the air being absorbed by the ocean, resulting in a change to the chemical balance of the water. This process begins when pollution such as automobile exhaust creates more carbon dioxide in the air than can be removed by plants and trees. When carbon dioxide dissolves into the ocean, it produces an increase of hydrogen in the water. This in turn produces water that contains less oxygen, creating an aquatic environment that will not support sea life.

Low-oxygen water creates areas in the ocean known as "dead zones." Without enough oxygen, plants and sea creatures suffocate and die. As Lubchenco explained, "The oceans are indeed becoming more acidic, as a result of absorbing carbon dioxide from the atmosphere, and that acidity represents a very real threat to much of the life in oceans, ranging from the smallest microscopic plants, to coral reefs, to things that form shells— mussels, oysters, clams—but even things like lobsters and crabs. We've only begun to scratch the surface in terms of really understanding the full range of the impacts of ocean acidifications, and it also affects physiology, not just the making of shells and skeletons."

> "We're changing the world in ways it's never been changed before, at faster rates and over larger scales, and we don't know the consequences. It's a massive experiment, and we don't know the outcome," Lubchenco claimed. "In the end, the decisions we make about the environment will be based on moral and ethical values. But those decisions will be much better decisions if they are in fact formed by the best possible science."

Lubchenco believes education is the first step in protecting the ocean from further acidification. "I think that oceans in general for many people are still out of sight, out of mind, and there is a lack of appreciation for how important the ocean is in the whole climate system, how important it is to people's everyday lives, and what the real risk is." Lubchenco hopes the NOAA can help to make more people aware of this unintended side effect of modern lifestyles. "When you think about the fact that half of Americans live in the coastal areas and the other half often goes there to play, we begin to appreciate the connectedness between the land and the ocean, and our lives and livelihoods and the environmental changes that are affecting the oceans and the land.

"Most Americans still believe that the oceans are so vast and bountiful that there is very little that we can do that would truly change them. The reality is that we are not just using oceans—we are using them up. If we truly want to be able to use them tomorrow, we have to do a better job of protecting them today," Lubchenco said. "The bottom line is, we're just dumping too many things into the ocean and we're taking too much out." For this reason, another of her main NOAA projects is the creation of marine reserves. A marine reserve is an aquatic version of the national parks and wilderness conservation areas that have been established on land. Marine reserves create "no take" areas in the ocean. In these areas, no fishing, mining, drilling, or dumping is allowed. Successful marine reserves have been maintained around the world for many years, but they are still relatively new in the U.S. "These fully protected marine reserves have been shown quite definitely to be extremely powerful in protecting habitat, in protecting biodiversity, and protecting the essential services provided by marine ecosystems," she argued. "And in some cases, they are also helping to replenish depleted fisheries. At present, far less than 1 percent of U.S. water is fully protected." Through the NOAA, Lubchenco plans to expand the number of marine reserves that exist in U.S. waters.

Lubchenco believes marine reserves are one way to start reversing the damage done to the environment. "Because we are capable of understanding what we're doing, it's appropriate for us to take stock of these changes and to ask what other choices we have," she explained. "If you asked most people how they depend on nature, they will focus on the things that we get—the food, the fiber, medicines, genes. But most people are unaware of the fact that ecosystems also provide services.… For example, forests provide flood control. They absorb water. They keep the water from just gushing downslope and causing floods.… The services by and large are outside our economic valuation system. We don't buy and sell and trade them. They're just there. We've always taken them for granted."

Looking to the Future

As she has done throughout her career, Lubchenco continues to look to science to provide solutions for critical environmental problems. In her role as head of the NOAA, she works to find practical ways to repair environmental damage and prevent further damage from being done. She prefers a balance of short- and long-term actions because she believes immediate changes provide people with a much-needed sense of confidence and hope for the future. "We're changing the world in ways it's never been changed before, at faster rates and over larger scales, and we don't know the consequences. It's a massive experiment, and we don't know the outcome,"

Lubchenco on an airboat tour of the Delta National Wildlife Refuge in Louisiana and other areas affected by the 2010 BP oil spill.

Lubchenco said. "In the end, the decisions we make about the environment will be based on moral and ethical values. But those decisions will be much better decisions if they are in fact formed by the best possible science."

"I think that what most members of the public are interested in is … will it affect me? Will it affect the things I care about? Can I do something about it?" But, she observed, "Nobody knows the definitive answers to these questions because we've never run this 'experiment' before. Human actions have inadvertently initiated a completely novel scenario. The real question is whether or not we wish to continue running this experiment."

MARRIAGE AND FAMILY

In 1971, Lubchenko married Bruce Menge, an ecologist and marine biology professor. They have two sons, Alexei, born in 1979, and Duncan, born in 1982.

HOBBIES AND OTHER INTERESTS

When she is not working, Lubchenco enjoys hiking, bird watching, traveling, dancing, and spending time with her family. She is interested in natural history and art and collecting ocean-inspired jewelry. Her favorite books include *Fragile Dominion* by Simon Levin, *Pine Island Paradox* by Kathleen Dean Moore, and *Arctic Dreams* by Barry Lopez. She loves being on or in the ocean and is happiest wading through mud and low tides, searching for marine life along the Pacific Ocean coastline.

HONORS AND AWARDS

Mercer Award (Ecological Society of America): 1979

Pew Scholar in Conservation and the Environment (Pew Charitable Trusts): 1992

MacArthur Fellowship (John D. and Catherine T. MacArthur Foundation): 1993

Heinz Award for the Environment (Heinz Family Philanthropies): 2002

Distinguished Service Award (Society for Conservation Biology): 2003

Nierenberg Award for Science in the Public Interest (Scripps Institution of Oceanography): 2003

Environmental Law Institute Award: 2004

Distinguished Scientist Award (American Institute of Biological Sciences): 2004

Public Understanding of Science and Technology Award (American Association for the Advancement of Science): 2005

Beijer Fellow of the Royal Swedish Academy of Sciences (Beijer Institute of Ecological Economics, Sweden): 2007

Zayed International Prize for the Environment (United Arab Emirates): 2008

FURTHER READING

Periodicals

Christian Science Monitor, Aug. 15, 1997, p.10; May 3, 2001, p.18

Nature, Mar. 26, 2009

New York Times, Dec. 23, 2008, p.3; Apr. 11, 2009, p.16

OnEarth, Summer 2007, p.8

Smithsonian, Apr. 2010, p.25

Online Articles

http://www.heinzawards.net
    (Heinz Awards, "Jane Lubchenco," undated)

http://www.nasonline.org
    (National Academy of Sciences, "InterViews: Jane Lubchenco," 2004)

http://www.nytimes.com/2009/03/24/science/earth/24prof.html
    (New York Times, "NOAA Chief Believes in Science as Social Contract," Mar. 24, 2009)

http://www.npr.org
   (NPR, "NOAA Head Jane Lubchenco on Ocean Policy," Mar. 27, 2009)
http://www.open-spaces.com
   (Open Spaces, "Earth's Unruly Tenant," Aug. 10, 2010)
http://e360.yale.edu
   (Yale Environment 360, "NOAA's New Chief on Restoring Science to
   U.S. Climate Policy," July 9, 2009)

ADDRESS

Jane Lubchenco
National Oceanic and Atmospheric Administration (NOAA)
1401 Constitution Ave. NW
Washington, DC 20230

WORLD WIDE WEB SITE

http://www.noaa.gov

Mike Lupica 1952-

American Journalist and Author
Nationally Syndicated Sports Columnist, TV Sports
Commentator, and Author of Popular Novels for
Young Adults

BIRTH

Michael Thomas Lupica (pronounced LOO-pik-uh) was born
on May 11, 1952, in Oneida, New York.

YOUTH

Lupica grew up in Nashua, New Hampshire. His father was
an enthusiastic sports fan who shared his love of sports with

his son. From a very young age, Lupica was enthralled with all aspects of sports. He and his father kept track of all kinds of statistics and scores and monitored the performances of professional teams and individual players. Sometimes the games they followed ran late into the evening, past Lupica's bedtime. Then his father would write notes about what happened after Lupica went to sleep. He would leave the notes for Lupica to read the next morning, so Lupica would always know right away what had happened in sports the night before.

> "I always tell anyone that wants to write, if there is a school paper, it is the greatest training ground in the world, because you would never want to embarrass yourself in front of your friends," Lupica recalled. "If your friends are reading your stuff, you've got to make it as good as you can."

Even as a child, Lupica knew he wanted to be a writer. He wanted to write about sports for a big newspaper, and maybe have his own sports column one day. And he also knew that he wanted to write books. Lupica started writing mystery stories when he was ten years old.

Lupica's first journalism experience was writing about sports for his high school newspaper. This was good writing practice, and it also led to his first paying job as a writer. "When I was in high school, I started writing for my school paper," he recalled. "I always tell anyone that wants to write, if there is a school paper, it is the greatest training ground in the world, because you would never want to embarrass yourself in front of your friends. If your friends are reading your stuff, you've got to make it as good as you can. Then I started covering my high school sports teams for my newspaper up in Nashua, New Hampshire—the *Nashua Telegraph*. I got five dollars a story, and I thought I was the richest guy in the world."

Lupica's love of sports wasn't limited to writing about it. In baseball, he played second base. He was also a point guard on his high school basketball team. "I think I still hold the New Hampshire high school record—I broke my glasses 14 times in my senior year." He also played golf and was a member of his high school cross country running team.

EDUCATION

By the time Lupica enrolled in Boston College, he was committed to a career as a writer. "I was writing for three school newspapers and working nights at the *Boston Globe*," he mentioned. "So I had clearly decided that this was what I wanted to do." During that time, Lupica also worked for several area newspapers. From 1970 to 1974, he was a sports correspondent for the *Boston Globe*, a large daily newspaper. From 1971 to 1975, he wrote a column for the *Boston Phoenix*, an arts and entertainment newsweekly, and sold some feature articles to the *Washington Star* daily newspaper in Washington, DC. Lupica graduated from Boston College in 1974.

CAREER HIGHLIGHTS

With a sports writing career spanning more than 30 years, Lupica has become one of the most well-known sports personalities in the U.S. His columns in the *New York Daily News* are reprinted in newspapers around the country. He is an anchor on "The Sports Reporters" talk show on ESPN and previously hosted "The Mike Lupica Show" on ESPN2. Lupica's blunt style and frequent rants about professional sports earned him the nickname "The Lip" and a reputation for being outspoken and unafraid to share his opinions. He doesn't mind if people agree with him or not. He explained that his reputation is "very liberating. I absolutely don't care what people think."

In addition to his career in sports journalism, Lupica is also the author of many books. He has written or contributed to a number of best-selling nonfiction books and has published a growing collection of popular novels for young adults. He manages these parallel careers by continuing to write his newspaper sports columns and appear on TV sports shows while working on his novels at the same time. Lupica has said that his successful career as both a sports columnist and an author is the fulfillment of the goal he set for himself in childhood.

Early Jobs

Although Lupica got his first paying job as a sports writer while he was still in high school, his professional career began after he graduated from college. In 1975, he began his first full-time job in sports journalism at the *New York Post* newspaper. There he was responsible for reporting on the NBA, particularly the New York Knicks basketball team. Lupica covered basketball for the *New York Post* for only a short time before he moved to the *New York Daily News* in 1977. At the *New York Daily News*, he became the youngest columnist ever to work at a major New York newspaper.

While continuing to write for the *New York Daily News*, Lupica also contributed stories to many different magazines. His writing appeared in many publications, including *World Tennis, Sport, Tennis, Golf Digest, Sports Illus-*

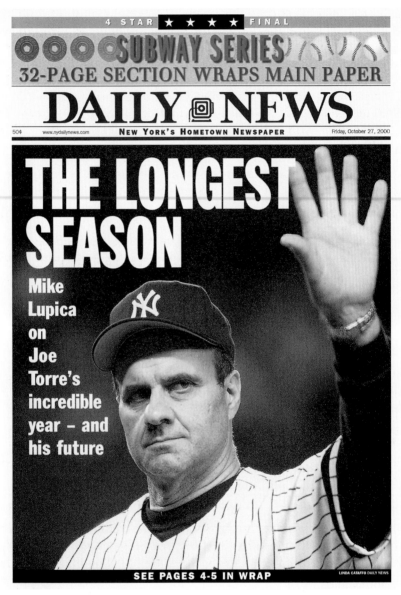

LINDA CATAFFO DAILY NEWS

As a sports journalist, Lupica has worked at the New York Daily News *since 1977.*

trated, *Men's Journal, Parade,* and *ESPN: The Magazine.* He created *Esquire* magazine's column "The Sporting Life" and wrote there for ten years.

During these years, Lupica brought his particular brand of sports journalism to television. He was a frequent guest on the TV news programs

"MacNeil-Lehrer NewsHour" and "Good Morning America." In 1982, he was a sports journalist for ESPN and also began appearing as a panelist on "The Sports Reporters." From 1982 to 1984 he was a sports reporter on the "CBS Morning News" program. Around this time, Lupica tried sports radio broadcasting, hosting a sports talk show on WNBC Radio. This lasted only a short time because he found that he really didn't care for the job. He later explained, "The function talk radio really seems to fulfill, is it's a place for people to [complain] and people will listen to them. It's anger 24 hours a day."

Becoming an Author

After working as a sports journalist for newspapers and TV for several years, Lupica began writing books as well. In the 1980s, he published three mystery novels for adults: *Dead Air* (1986), *Extra Credits* (1988), and *Limited Partner* (1990). All three books feature Peter Finley, an investigative reporter for a New York City cable TV station. In each book, Finley finds himself immersed in an investigation into murder where only he can find the truth. His first book, *Dead Air,* was nominated for an Edgar Allan Poe Award for Best First Mystery; Lupica later wrote a screenplay based on *Dead Air* that became the CBS TV movie *Money, Power, Murder.*

Lupica also published several non-fiction books related to sports journalism. He co-wrote autobiographies with baseball player Reggie Jackson (*Reggie: The Autobiography,* 1984) and NFL football coach Bill Parcells (*Parcells: Autobiography of the Biggest Giant of Them All,* 1987). He also collaborated with noted author and screenwriter William Goldman on *Wait 'Till Next Year: The Story of a Season When What Should've Happened Didn't, and What Could've Gone Wrong Did* (1988), a look at one year in New York City sports. He reprinted several of his most popular pieces in the 1988 book *Shooting from the Lip: Essays, Columns, Quips, and Gripes in the Grand Tradition of Dyspeptic Sports Writing.* In 1996, Lupica published the book *Mad as Hell: How Sports Got Away from the Fans—And How We Get It Back.* This nonfiction book presents his criticism of the professional sports industry. In writing about the complaints of many die-hard sports fans, he attacks such problems as greedy team owners, overpaid players, and the high price of tickets for live sporting events. A *Booklist* reviewer declared that disgruntled sports fans "will enjoy sputtering angrily as they read this litany of wrongdoing."

Lupica's next sports-related non-fiction book was *Summer of '98: When Homers Flew, Records Fell, and Baseball Reclaimed America,* published in 1999. This book combined the dramatic story of the 1998 professional

*Since 1982, Lupica has appeared regularly on the weekly ESPN program
"The Sports Reporters," where several sports commentators discuss
the week's news. He's shown here with (from left) Mitch Albom,
Israel Gutierrez, and John Saunders.*

baseball season with personal stories about Lupica and his young sons. During that season, he and his sons followed the ongoing competition between Mark McGwire and Sammy Sosa as the two star hitters raced to break the record for most home runs in one season. "The book is about the home-run chase and about how baseball came into my sons' lives this summer ... when the home runs were landing in our living room." *Publishers Weekly* called it "A feel-great book.... [Lupica] gives himself completely over to the beauty of baseball as both a game and as an agent of bonding between fathers and children."

Lupica soon combined his interest in writing novels with his love for sports in several new novels for adults. These books—set in the worlds of basketball, football, and baseball—provide an insider's view of professional sports. In *Jump* (1995), investigative attorney Mike DiMaggio must discover the truth when two professional basketball players are accused of rape. In *Bump and Run* (2000) Lupica introduced Jack Malloy, who unexpectedly inherits a professional football team when his father dies suddenly. In spite of his complete lack of experience, Malloy is determined to take his team to the Super Bowl. In *Full Court Press* (2001), talented Delilah "Dee" Gerard becomes the first woman to play in the NBA. Used as a marketing gimmick by the team owner and largely ignored by her teammates, Gerard also struggles with a vindictive sports writer intent on discovering scandals from her past. In *Wild Pitch* (2002), retired pitcher Charlie Stoddard returns for one last season on the mound, only to stir up conflict with his son—also a pitcher on the same team.

Lupica returned to the world of Jack Malloy with *Red Zone* (2003), a sequel to *Bump and Run*. Malloy has lost ownership of his team, but he continues to scheme to regain control and bring the team back on track, despite the interference of his twin sons. In *Too Far* (2004), former sports writer Ben Mitchell investigates the mysterious death of a high school basketball coach. When Mitchell uncovers what looks like evidence of violent hazing activities, he suddenly finds that there are some people who will do anything to prevent the truth from being revealed.

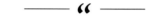

"Sports teaches kids about being on a team, being part of something greater than themselves if they play hard and well and unselfishly. If they can learn that, they can apply it to anything they do, in or out of sports, for the rest of their lives."

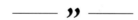

Writing for Young Adults

In 2004, Lupica published his first novel for young adult readers. *Travel Team* is the story of Danny Walker, who is 12 years old and in love with the game of basketball. Danny has natural talent and a drive to succeed, but finds that he is too short to qualify for the middle school basketball team. When Danny's father, a former professional basketball player, learns that his son didn't make the school team, he starts up a new team to give kids like Danny a chance to play. Danny's father turns out to be a highly competitive coach, and Danny struggles with the pros and cons of playing on his father's team. Ultimately Danny must decide how important basketball really is, and whether he wants to devote his life to the sport like his father did.

In writing *Travel Team*, Lupica drew on his own experiences as a youth basketball coach. "My middle son got cut from his seventh grade boys travel basketball team, along with another boy, for being too small. I started a team for all the kids that got cut. I hired a coach. We had a season. It turned out to be a tremendous experience, and that gave me the bare bones of the idea for *Travel Team*."

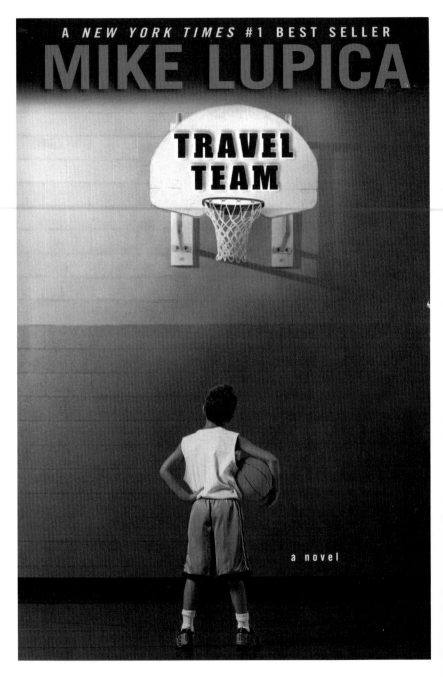

After writing several books for adults, Lupica wrote Travel Team, *his first novel for young adults and the first of many books that have featured kids dealing with real-life issues within the context of stories about sports.*

Travel Team became the first of many novels written for young adults that have been widely praised for their deep knowledge of sports, interesting characters, believable family situations, and compelling stories. "Lupica has great respect for the boys struggling to deal with their own skills, their fathers, their teammates, and their coaches," Claire Rosser wrote in *Kliatt.* "All the details of basketball games and practices will be welcome to true basketball fans. It's such a relief to have a sports tale written by someone who truly understands the game—and Lupica knows how to create believable characters as well. An excellent sports story." That view was echoed in *Kirkus Reviews.* "[Lupica] has the knowledge of the game and the lean prose to make this a taut, realistic story not just about the game but about heart, character, and family. A winner."

Lupica's next young adult novel, *Heat* (2006), focuses on 12-year-old Michael and 17-year-old Carlos Arroyo, two Cuban-American brothers recently orphaned by their father's sudden death. In order to avoid being separated in foster care, the boys pretend that their father is still alive. They tell everyone that their father is visiting relatives in Miami so they can stay together in their apartment until Carlos turns 18. The plan seems to work until Michael is challenged by some of the other Little League coaches, who suspect that he is too old for Little League because of his strength and talent as a top-notch pitcher. Just when things seem to be falling apart, heroes emerge from unexpected places. "Lupica wrings plenty of genuine emotion from the melodramatic frame story ... by building characters who speak for themselves, not the author, and by enlivening the story with a teen version of street humor," raved Bill Ott in *Booklist.* "The dialogue crackles, and the rich cast of supporting characters—especially Michael's battery mate, catcher, and raconteur Manny—nearly steals the show. Top-notch entertainment."

In *Miracle on 49th Street* (2006), Lupica tells the story of 12-year-old Molly Parker, who loves basketball mostly because her father is Josh Cameron, star player for Boston Celtics. Molly was raised in England by her mother, who never told Josh that he had a daughter. After her mother dies, Molly finds Josh and tells him that he is her father. The plot unfolds as Josh and Molly get to know each other and grow into their new relationship. "Lupica creates intriguing, complex characters in Molly, Sam, and Josh, and he paces his story well, with enough twists and cliff-hangers to keep the pages turning," Jeffrey A. French wrote in *School Library Journal.* "This is an entertaining work."

Lupica returned to the characters of *Travel Team* with the 2007 sequel *Summer Ball.* The story opens with Danny still waiting for his growth spurt as he sets off for summer basketball camp. Worrying that everyone at camp will be bigger and better than him, Danny quickly finds camp life complicated by a coach who seems to have a problem with him. Danny again questions whether he should just quit basketball for good. But then he discovers that there might be a reason why the coach doesn't like him, and it might have something to do with Danny's father. "*Summer Ball* is a great stand-alone novel," Sarah Sawtelle noted in a review for TeenReads.com. "With humor and fast action both on and off the court, this is a summer read not to be missed."

―――― " ――――

"Sports teaches kids about being on a team, being part of something greater than themselves if they play hard and well and unselfishly," Lupica argued. *"If they can learn that, they can apply it to anything they do, in or out of sports, for the rest of their lives."*

―――― " ――――

Published in 2008, *The Big Field* is a young adult baseball story starring 14-year-old Keith "Hutch" Hutchinson. Hutch plays second base and is the captain of his American Legion team. But the real star of the team is his friend Darryl "D-Will" Williams, a top shortstop. Hutch is a solid player, but knows he could be better with the help of his father, a former amateur baseball star. But his father's disappointment with his own failures prevents him from helping his son. Just as Hutch's team is about to make it to the state championships, Hutch finds out that his father has been training with Darryl instead of him. "Vivid descriptions of pivotal inning and plays, snappy dialogue, and realistic conflicts propel the characters and the story toward the state finals and a father-son breakthrough," reviewer Berry Larson wrote in *School Library Journal.* "Baseball fans will revel in Lupica's exciting sports commentary and Hutch's competitive spirit and emotional highs and lows."

In *The Million Dollar Throw* (2009), 13-year-old Nate Brodie has finally saved up enough money to buy the autographed football he's wanted. But something completely unexpected comes along with the football—a chance to win a million dollars. All he has to do is throw a pass through a target at a New England Patriots game. Nate should be excited but instead, all he feels is pressure. His dad lost his job and the family is about to lose their home. Winning the prize money would make everything okay again. Except that Nate suddenly finds he's lost his talent for making pin-point passes. Will he be able to make the throw of a lifetime? A reviewer for *Horn*

Book said *The Million Dollar Throw* has "plenty of fast-paced football details for sports fans in this story propelled by the strength of family, friendship, and team."

In *The Batboy* (2010), Lupica tells the story of 14-year-old Brian Dudley, who has just landed his dream summer job: batboy for his favorite team, the Detroit Tigers. For Brian, the job means more than a chance to hang around with his baseball idols. Brian hopes to understand some things about his father, who chose baseball over Brian and his mother. As the summer progresses, Brian develops an unlikely friendship with Hank Bishop, a disgraced baseball player trying to rebuild his career. Brian and Hank each find what they were looking for, although not in the ways they expected. "Lupica is at the top of his game, crafting a crisp, fast-paced novel teeming with edge-of-the-seat baseball drama," reviewer Marilyn Taniguchi wrote in *School Library Journal.* "Though this novel will undoubtedly appeal to those who equate summer with baseball, it should also win over readers who appreciate finely crafted storytelling and engaging characters.

The "Comeback Kids" Series

In 2007, Lupica decided to begin writing the "Comeback Kids" series, a new series of sports novels aimed at slightly younger readers. The first book in the series was *Hot Hand*, the story of ten-year-old Billy and his life on and off the basketball court. Billy's life hasn't been so good since his parents divorced. His mother works long hours and takes a lot of business trips. His father moved out of the family home but still coaches Billy's basketball team and is as hard on Billy as ever. Billy's younger brother Ben has been growing more and more quiet since the divorce and doesn't seem interested in anything. To make matters worse, Ben is being bullied at school and Billy has to be the one to handle it. When the family is thrown into turmoil, Billy must be the one to find a solution that works for everyone.

Two-Minute Drill, another "Comeback Kids" book published in 2007, focuses on two sixth grade football players with completely different talents. Scott is a straight-A student, but is not very good at football. Chris is the star quarterback and the most popular kid in school, but is not very good at his schoolwork—dyslexia makes him a poor student. The two boys discover that they each have a secret, and they become friends as the story unfolds. In facing their own challenges, Scott and Chris both discover that the will to succeed is sometimes more important than natural ability.

Lupica published two more "Comeback Kids" books in 2008. In *Long Shot*, Pedro Morales is a model point guard. Always content with helping others

The Comeback Kids novels are geared to slightly younger readers but still focus on sports themes.

look great, Pedro's job on the basketball court is to set up his teammates to score. When Pedro decides to run for class president, he soon learns that he will be going up against Ned, the star forward and also the most popular boy in school. For once, Pedro wants to win something great for himself. But he learns the hard way that being a good teammate doesn't always mean that others will return the favor. *Safe at Home* tells the story of Nick Crandall, who feels like he doesn't belong anywhere. He certainly doesn't feel at home with his new foster parents. They are both college professors who know nothing about sports. Nick is a star athlete but not much of a student. He is good enough to make the varsity baseball team even though he's only 12 years old, but his teammates aren't interested in having a little kid for a catcher. Before everyone realizes he's in the wrong place, Nick wants to figure out how to prove that he belongs.

In 2010, Lupica published *Shoot-Out,* a Comeback Kids book that looks at what happens when a star player ends up on the worst team in the league. Jake loves soccer and had been a member of the championship team. When he finds himself playing for the last place team, he realizes that if he doesn't want to quit soccer, he has to learn to lose. Jake struggles to maintain a positive attitude while his team is trounced in every game. Ultimately, Jake's teammate Kevin shows him that good sportsmanship is equally important on and off the field.

According to reviewers, the "Comeback Kids" books feature many of the same characteristics that have made Lupica's books for older readers so compelling: fast-paced stories, interesting characters, meaty plots, and realistic sports action. "[*Shoot-Out* is] an enjoyable sports story with lots of action," Todd Morning wrote in *Booklist.* "[*Long Shot*] sends kids a message about the importance of cooperation and teamwork both on and off the court, without being preachy and didactic," Amy Joslyn wrote in *School Library Journal.* "This brisk story of friendship and football will be a huge hit with the target audience," a writer for *Kirkus Reviews* said about *Two-Minute Drill.*

Trying Something New

In 2010, Lupica published a book that was different from his earlier writings: *Hero,* his first young adult book that is not about sports. *Hero* imagines what happens when 14-year-old Zach Harriman begins to develop super powers. After his father's sudden death, Zach gradually discovers that he has new abilities. He can move from one place to another as fast as a text message travels. He can become invisible. He has incredible strength, sharpened senses, and a strange need to patrol New York City's Central

Park at night. And he can fly. Zach doesn't understand these new powers or why he has them. Slowly he learns that it might have something to do with his father's death. Zach knew his dad had been a hero who saved America. What Zach didn't know was that his dad was a superhero, and now it's Zach's turn to take up the battle against evil. "In a major departure from his YA sports fiction," Richard Luzer wrote in *School Library Journal*, "the popular Lupica opts for a high-concept, high-octane action thriller." A reviewer for *Publishers Weekly* offered another view, calling Hero "a moving tale of adolescent growth."

———— **"** ————

"All my books, at some point, are about the things that I think are the most important, which are friendship and loyalty and also the ability to get back up after you get knocked down a little," Lupica concluded. *"Anybody can get knocked down in life or in sports. . . . It's how you get back up that is a measure of your heart and your character and your spirit. So I hope people always take that message away from my books."*

———— **"** ————

Lupica explained why he decided to write a non-sports book. "I always thought about what it would be like if I took a kid and gave him superpowers. Then, when my editor found out that I liked comic books, he asked me the eternal superhero question: 'If you could fly or be invisible, which would you be?' I said fly and I thought flying would always win hands down, but I was surprised to find that when I asked different groups the answer always came out 50/50. So having a kid with both powers was my jumping off point for this book."

Lupica plans to continue his dual careers as a sports journalist and a novelist. He continues to appear as a commentator on TV sports shows and to write for the *New York Daily News*. There, his Sunday column "Shooting from the Lip" has become a staple of New York journalism, supplemented by his Monday column, "Mondays with Mike," and his web-only column, all known for their strong opinions, exclusive interviews, and insightful observations.

But Lupica also enjoys writing novels for young readers and already has some new stories in mind. He has said that he likes writing sports fiction because "sports teaches kids about being on a team, being part of something greater than themselves if they play hard and well and unselfishly. If they can learn that, they can apply it to anything they do, in or out of

Lupica reading his book Long Shot *to sixth graders from a
New York City middle school.*

sports, for the rest of their lives." However, he is not ruling out the possibility of writing more non-sports books. "All my books, at some point, are about the things that I think are the most important, which are friendship and loyalty and also the ability to get back up after you get knocked down a little," he concluded. "Anybody can get knocked down in life or in sports. That doesn't show anybody anything about you. But it's how you get back up that is a measure of your heart and your character and your spirit. So I hope people always take that message away from my books."

For young people who are interested in a writing career, Lupica's advice is to get started as soon as possible. "If you want to write, and that is your passion and dream, just write as much as you can," he stressed. "If there is a school paper, write for that. Keep a journal. Write observations about the world. The first time that you write a story that you are proud of and somebody wants to read it, you're a writer. Another way to get better as a writer is to read. There is still no microchip, technology, cable remote, iPod, or video game that can do what a good story does. It takes you to a world that you may have never inhabited on your own. That is more magic to me than anything that a computer can do."

HOBBIES AND OTHER INTERESTS

Lupica enjoys all sports, but his favorite is baseball. "There is nothing I like better than taking my kids and sitting in a ballpark on a nice day and eating popcorn and watching baseball." In his spare time, he likes to play tennis and golf. Lupica also coaches youth sports, including basketball, soccer, and Little League baseball. He claimed that he follows the coaching plan he learned from his friend Paul Westphal, a former NBA player and coach:

1. If you're open, shoot.
2. If somebody else is more open, pass him the ball and let him shoot.
3. Have fun.

"I tell the kids all the time, this ain't a job, this is playing ball with your buddies, and if you can't do it with a smile on your face, we're all wasting our time."

MARRIAGE AND FAMILY

Lupica married his wife Taylor in 1986. They have three sons, Christopher, Alex, and Zach, and one daughter, Hannah. Lupica lives with his family in New Canaan, Connecticut.

SELECTED WRITINGS

Young Adult Novels

Travel Team, 2004
Heat, 2006
Miracle on 49th Street, 2006
Summer Ball, 2007
The Big Field, 2008
Million Dollar Throw, 2009
The Batboy, 2010
Hero, 2010

Comeback Kids Novels

Hot Hand, 2007
Two-Minute Drill, 2007
Long Shot, 2008
Safe at Home, 2008
Shoot-Out, 2010

Other Writings

Reggie: The Autobiography, 1984 (with Reggie Jackson)
Dead Air, 1986
Parcells: Autobiography of the Biggest Giant of Them All, 1987 (with Bill Parcells)
Extra Credits, 1988
Shooting from the Lip: Essays, Columns, Quips, and Gripes in the Grand Tradition of Dyspeptic Sports Writing, 1988
Wait 'Till Next Year: The Story of a Season When What Should've Happened Didn't, and What Could've Gone Wrong Did, 1988 (with William Goldman)
Limited Partner, 1990
Jump, 1995
Mad as Hell: How Sports Got Away from the Fans—And How We Get It Back, 1996
Summer of '98: When Homers Flew, Records Fell, and Baseball Reclaimed America, 1999
Bump and Run, 2000
Full Court Press, 2001
Wild Pitch, 2002
Red Zone, 2003
Too Far, 2004

HONORS AND AWARDS

Jim Murray Award (National Football Foundation): 2003
New York Sportswriter of the Year (National Sportscasters and Sportwriters Association): 2010

FURTHER READING

Periodicals

Christian Science Monitor, May 13, 1999, p.18
Connecticut Post, May 29, 2007
Denver Post, Nov. 16, 2009, p.A17
South Florida Sun-Sentinel, June 6, 2006, p.E2
USA Today, Nov. 7, 2000, p.C3

Online Articles

http://www.huffingtonpost.com/mike-lupica/we-still-love-a-good-stor_b
_352862.html
  (Huffington Post, "We Still Love a Good Story," Nov. 11, 2009)
http://www.tampabay.com
  (St. Petersburg Times/Tampa Bay.com, "Sportswriter Mike Lupica Writes
  Young Adult Novels with Message: Character Counts," Nov. 14, 2010)
http://www.teenreads.com/authors
  (Teen Reads, "Author Profile: Mike Lupica," no date)
http://www.timeforkids.com
  (Time for Kids, "Catching Up with Mike Lupica," May 7, 2010)

ADDRESS

Mike Lupica
Penguin Group USA
375 Hudson St.
New York, NY 10014

WORLD WIDE WEB SITE

http://www.mikelupicabooks.com

Charles Martinet 1955-

American Actor
Voice of Mario and Other Nintendo Characters

BIRTH

Charles Martinet was born on September 17, 1955, in San Jose, California. He has sometimes spelled his last name Martinee or Martinez in his acting credits.

YOUTH

Martinet's family moved to Spain when he was 12 years old. They later lived in France. As a result, he learned to speak both Spanish and French fluently. He also speaks a little Italian.

EDUCATION

Martinet attended the American School of Paris, located in the Parisian suburb of Saint-Cloud. As a young adult, his ambition was to become a lawyer. When he was about 20 years old, however, a friend convinced him to take a drama class. He loved it and immediately decided to drop out of college in order to pursue a professional acting career. He auditioned for, and won, an apprenticeship at the Berkeley Repertory Theater, a famous and respected community theater in California. After spending some time there, he went to England to study at the Drama Studio London. He then returned to California, where he continued acting. "My parents have always been incredibly supportive; they put me through college, then [I] left college and then they put me through drama school," Martinet acknowledged. "They helped me get started and it's been nothing but love and support."

> "My parents have always been incredibly supportive; they put me through college, then [I] left college and then they put me through drama school," Martinet acknowledged. "They helped me get started and it's been nothing but love and support."

FIRST JOBS

Martinet was involved with some 75 plays in London and California. Among them were several plays written by William Shakespeare, a 16th-century playwright considered by many to be the world's greatest. Those acting jobs helped him years later: he used his experience playing one of the Shakespearean characters to inspire his work in video games.

Making Corporate Videos

Martinet's next career move was to become involved in the world of corporate videos. For the most part, these videos are never seen by the general public. Instead, they present information about a business or company to possible partners, customers, or clients. Corporate videos are an important business tool, and large companies may spend a lot of money producing them. They can be serious or humorous in tone. Martinet has appeared in more than 500 of these videos, many of them for such major companies as Apple Computers, Microsoft, and IBM. He sometimes filled the role of a serious narrator, while at other times, he played such characters as an engineer, a crazy scientist, a cowboy, or a geek. In addition, he portrayed these characters live at trade shows, where business people come to learn about other businesses.

CAREER HIGHLIGHTS

Audition of a Lifetime

One day in 1987, Martinet was relaxing at the beach when he got a message from a friend, urging him to go to an audition for a trade show. Martinet didn't really want to leave the beach, but he finally did go to the audition—arriving just as the crew was preparing to leave. "I said, 'Excuse me, can I please read for this?'" he remembered. "The producer looked at his watch, said, 'OK. You're an Italian plumber from Brooklyn and we've got this animation system, and we're not sure it's even going to work yet, and you'll have this stuff glued to your face and the cartoon character will move when you talk.'" Video games were still fairly new at the time, based mainly on simple movements and actions. The very idea of a game with a storyline was somewhat surprising to Martinet, and there was no picture of the character to inspire him.

"It's never been done before and in any case if it doesn't work you still gotta talk to people. So make up a video game, make up an accent and start talking to people," the producer told him. The actor's first idea was to use a stereotypical, gruff New York accent for the character, but the producer had told him the game was supposed to be appealing to all ages. He searched in his mind for a voice that would be more appropriate for young children, something softer and gentler. He had played an old Italian man named Gemio in Shakespeare's *The Taming of the Shrew,* and Gemio suddenly came back to him as he prepared to audition. Making the old man's voice younger and more energetic, he turned to the camera and started talking.

"I said, 'Hello, it's a-me, Mario! Okey dokey, let's make a pizza pie together! You a-gonna get some sauces. I'm-a gonna get some spaghetti. We're gonna put the spaghetti and the sauces into the pizza. Then we're gonna make lasagna. Then we're gonna make spaghetti and meatballs! Ooh, mama mia, I'm getting hungry!'" Martinet remembered. "I don't know what I said, but I talked and I talked for 30 minutes or longer, until I heard 'Cut! Stop! We have no more tape! Thank you. We'll be in touch.'" He didn't find that reassuring, because he knew that "we'll be in touch" often really means "you will not be called back" at auditions. In this case, however, Martinet's tape was such a standout that it was the only one sent to Nintendo for approval. He was soon hired to give life to the Mario character at the trade show.

Martinet voiced the character of Mario at trade shows for several years before technology advanced enough to allow voices in video games. The first game to feature Martinet as Mario was Super Mario 64 *in 1996.*

Origins of Mario

Mario had first appeared in an early video arcade game called *Donkey Kong,* created by Shigeru Miyamoto for the Nintendo company. (For more information on Miyamoto, see *Biography Today Scientists and Inventors,* Vol. 5.) *Donkey Kong* was the first game to have characters acting out a simple story, which had been developed before the technical aspects of the game. The plot had Donkey Kong, a huge ape, kidnapping a girl named Pauline. The third character was a carpenter who had to overcome various obstacles in order to rescue Pauline from Donkey Kong. His outstanding power was his ability to jump over gaps, and he had to do this repeatedly in order to foil Donkey Kong. The character was known as Jumpman, but he had the big hat, bushy mustache, and blue overalls that Mario still wears today.

Jumpman was so popular that Nintendo began developing a new game that would feature him. That game was *Mario Bros.,* and it was released in 1983. Jumpman now had a real name: Mario. It was chosen because of the character's resemblance to Mario Segale, the landlord of Nintendo's warehouse in Redmond, Washington. Mario had also been transformed from a carpenter to a plumber, and he had been given a brother named Luigi to help him defeat nasty creatures down in New York City's sewer system. In 1985, a sequel called *Super Mario Bros.* was released, and for many years it was the top-selling video game in the industry. *Super Mario Bros.* first saw Mario and Luigi battling against Bowser, navigating the Mushroom Kingdom, and trying to save Princess Peach—all of which became recurring elements in later updates of the *Mario Bros.* games.

Actor in a Box

Computer memory was limited in the early days of video games, so it wasn't possible to have Mario speak during his first years. At the trade show Martinet auditioned for, however, Nintendo was going to use advanced technology that would allow him to give life to Mario, while hiding in a soundproof box with a complex computer system. A mold was made of the actor's face, and a mask produced from the mold. Contact wires were glued and taped to his face and connected to the processing system.

When everything was in place, the system was supposed to translate Martinet's speech and facial expressions to an animated Mario appearing on a monitor a short distance away. Martinet would be able to see the people who were looking at the monitor, but they wouldn't be able to see him. He could have real-time conversations with them and it would seem exactly as if Mario was speaking to them. The people at Nintendo hoped that all

Martinet with Mario and Luigi, two of the Nintendo characters he voices.

the equipment would work correctly and hold up until the conclusion of the trade show. It was so hot in the box that the glue and tape on Martinet's face began to melt. The system kept working, however, and Martinet was a huge success as the voice and personality of Mario. He has continued to play Mario at trade shows for more than 20 years.

It was a major step forward for video games and for Martinet's career when technology advanced enough to allow Mario to speak a little more in his games. Martinet first provided the voice of Mario for a Nintendo game with *Super Mario 64*, which was first released in Japan on June 23, 1996. In addition to enhanced sound capability, *Super Mario 64* had 3-D graphics and became one of the world's best-selling video games. It is still ranked by many gamers as one of the best games of all time.

Voice of Nintendo

The Mario character went on to appear in more than 200 games produced by Nintendo, both in starring roles and minor parts, as the company continued to develop and use the newest technological innovations. Mario has appeared in virtually every gaming platform, from arcade games to Wii. Mario titles include *Mario Kart, Super Smash Bros., Super Mario Sunshine, Mario Golf, Mario Party,* and many more. The little plumber has become the symbol of the entire Nintendo company.

Every time he voices Mario, Martinet keeps the character light, positive, fun, and upbeat, no matter what challenges or enemies he has to face. Mario is known for his playful shouts of "Wa-hoo!" and "Mamma mia!" Martinet continues to be the voice of Mario in games and in real-time appearances, but he is also the voice of many other major Nintendo characters as well, including Mario's brother Luigi, Baby Mario, Mario's enemy Wario, Waluigi, Toadsworth, and others.

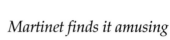

Martinet finds it amusing that millions of people around the world have heard his voice, but he can usually walk down the street completely unnoticed. "There is a certain level of wonderfulness that comes with being a celebrity without fame," he said.

The process of developing a game from start to finish is a long one. Martinet's part in any new Mario game is very important, but in the overall picture, it doesn't take much time. Sometimes he is sent video of the game beforehand, so he can think about how he might like to have the character react to certain situations. At other times, he has no idea what the game will look like until it's time to record. In the first games he voiced, only very small sound bites could be used, but as technology advanced, Mario's personality and vocabulary has grown, too. A script is provided, but Martinet does a lot of improvising. In the end, the best takes are sent to Nintendo for final approval by Shigeru Miyamoto, who makes the ultimate choice about what is used.

Improved technology has drastically changed the experience of performing as Mario, Wario, and other characters in real-time situations. Computers have become so much more powerful and efficient that Martinet no longer has to be cooped up in a hot, soundproofed box, or to have equipment taped or glued to his face. He does still travel and make live appearances, but now it is also possible for him to sit in his own home and give life to Mario and other Nintendo characters at locations that are thousands of miles away, and he often does this. "I sit there in my little bunny shoes in the morning, and just talk with people at the Nintendo World Store, or anywhere in the world," he said.

Life beyond Mario

Providing voices for Mario and his companions is certainly Martinet's best-known job, but he continues to do many others. He has supplied voices for many other video games, including those for companies competing with Nintendo. He can be heard in the "Carmen Sandiego" and "Star Wars" games, and in *Slave Zero, Uprising, Cel Damage, Space Quest 6: The Final Frontier,* and many others. He also lends his voice to educational software. In "The Cat in the Hat" educational software, Martinet plays the Cat and Yertle the Turtle. In the popular "Reader Rabbit" series, which helps children learn reading, math, and other skills, he plays Reader Rabbit in the English, French, and Spanish versions of the programs. He is also the voice of the Leapfrog Express line of educational toys, recognizable by his friendly invitation, "Ribbit ribbit, let's play!" More than 100 educational games and toys feature Martinet's voice.

> "
>
> *Martinet has created hundreds of characters, but he says that Mario is definitely his favorite. "For me, it's a perfect marriage because Mario and I have so much in common—joy, fun, laughter, life adventure. I bring that aspect of myself to Mario. It seems to work."*
>
> "

Martinet has also done voice work for television and radio. He has played over 100 characters in animated features for Sony Wonderfilm and Hallmark Cartoons, including King Arthur, Moses, and Tarzan. He has also played small parts as a regular actor in the films *The Game* and *Nine Months,* as well as the television movie *The Last of His Tribe.* He has appeared in television programs, including "Nash Bridges" and "Midnight Caller."

Although he enjoys all kinds of acting and performing, Martinet says that voice acting is a special kind of fun. He finds it amusing that while millions of people around the world have heard his voice, he can usually walk down the street and be completely unnoticed. "There is a certain level of wonderfulness that comes with being a celebrity without fame," he said.

Martinet gets ideas for his characters by watching people, studying their movements and mannerisms, and listening to their speech patterns. He commented that voice acting requires good general health. "I try to take care of my whole body by keeping in shape," he explained. "I try to eat well and get a good night's sleep. It's important to drink lots of water and not a lot of dairy products because you want to keep your throat nice and

*Mario and the gang have continued to appear in Nintendo games on each
new gaming platform, including Wii.*

clear. You also have to laugh and smile a lot and I don't scream too much
because that really strains the vocal folds."

When all his work is taken into consideration, this versatile actor has created hundreds of characters, but he says that Mario is definitely his favorite. "For me, it's a perfect marriage because Mario and I have so much
in common—joy, fun, laughter, life adventure. I bring that aspect of myself
to Mario. It seems to work." He feels the public loves Mario because the
little plumber "loves life, loves adventure, jumps over challenges and finds
a way to get through. He always moves forward in a positive way."

Mario may not be a very complex character, but even after more than 20
years, Martinet doesn't find it dull playing him. "I never get bored," he

129

said. "It is so much fun to do and to see what new things are going to come out of the genius that is Mr. Miyamoto and the incredible team at Nintendo. Talking to fans and seeing their enthusiasm and the wonderful impact the games have on people will always bring me joy."

MAJOR INFLUENCES

Martinet says that one of his greatest inspirations in life is Mario himself. "He has a positive attitude to life and is never cynical. If I could be anyone it would be Mario."

HOBBIES AND OTHER INTERESTS

Martinet enjoys playing video games, and his favorites are those featuring Mario, especially *Mario Kart.* Some of his favorite actors are Robin Williams, Robert De Niro, and Colin Firth.

SELECTED CREDITS

Movies

Last of His Tribe, 1992 (TV movie)
Nine Months, 1995
The Game, 1997

Video Games

Space Quest 6: The Final Frontier, 1995
Super Mario Bros. 64, 1996
Mario Kart 64, 1996
Uprising, 1997
Mario Party, 1998
Slave Zero, 1999
Mario Golf, 1999
Mario Party 3, 2000
Super Mario World, 2001
Cel Damage, 2001
Super Mario Sunshine, 2002
Mario vs. Donkey Kong, 2004
Super Mario 64 DS, 2004
Mario Superstar Basketball, 2005
Mario Kart DS, 2005
Super Smash Bros. Brawl, 2008
Mario Kart Wii, 2008
Resonance of Fate, 2010
Super Mario Galaxy 2, 2010

FURTHER READING

Periodicals

Sunday Herald Sun (Melbourne, Australia), Oct. 13, 2002, p.F3

Online Articles

http://www.bbc.co.uk/newsbeat/10283772
  (BBC Newsbeat, "Mamma Mia! It's the Voice of Mario!" June 11, 2010)
http://www.cubed3.com
  (Cubed3, "Interview with Charles Martinet," Dec. 7, 2003)
http://www.gamervision.com
  (Gamervision, "Charles Martinet on Being the Voice of Mario," June 2,
  2010)
http://www.n-sider.com
  (N-Sider, "Charles Martinet Down Under," Nov. 14, 2002)
http://www.wii-kombo.com
  (Wii Kombo, David Oxford, "Charles Martinet Celebrates 15 Years of
  Wario with Kombo," Sep. 15, 2008)

ADDRESS

Charles Martinet
CAM Creative Service
603 Main Street
Sausalito, CA 94965-2318

WORLD WIDE WEB SITE

http://www.charlesmartinet.com

Bridgit Mendler 1992-

American Actress

Star of the Disney Channel TV Program "Good Luck Charlie"

BIRTH

Bridgit Claire Mendler was born on December 18, 1992, in Washington, DC. She has a brother, Nicolas, and a sister, Zoey.

YOUTH AND EDUCATION

In 2000, when Mendler was eight years old, the family moved to Mill Valley, California, which is near San Francis-

———— " ————

Mendler decided early on that she wanted to act. "I was finishing up one play that I was working on through the community theater program, and I came up to her and I said, 'Mommy, this is what I want to do!'" she recalled. "It seems like that was about right, because I've kept up with it."

———— " ————

co. Her family chose not to have a television for several years, so she and her siblings had to learn other ways to keep themselves entertained. "I liked hanging out with the other kids," she recalled. "I liked reading. I was crazy about the Harry Potter books." While she was in the second grade, she took part in a school play about mathematics, in the role of Princess Multiplication. She enjoyed the experience so much that she started attending drama camps and being involved with other local theater productions.

Mendler decided early on that she wanted to stick with acting. "My mom actually remembers, and I don't remember this," she said. "But I was finishing up one play that I was working on through the community theater program, and I came up to her and I said, 'Mommy, this is what I want to do!' I don't remember saying that, but apparently I said that. It seems like that was about right, because I've kept up with it."

Mendler has adapted her education to suit her growing career as an actor. She attends high school online through the Education Program for Gifted Youth at Stanford University.

FIRST JOBS

As a child, Mendler worked in many local theater productions in the San Francisco Bay Area. She eventually became the youngest performer ever in the San Francisco Fringe Festival, a respected theater festival that is held yearly.

Signing with a Talent Agent

Mendler's parents were very supportive of her acting ambitions, and by the time she was 11 years old, she had signed with a talent agent. She did voice acting for the animated film *The Legend of Buddha*, released in 2004. It told the story of the founder of Buddhism, from his youthful days through his quest for spiritual enlightenment. It was nominated for an Academy Award for best animated feature film. Following that, she played the part

Mendler (left) in a scene from The Clique.

of Thorn in the video game *Bone: The Great Cow Race,* which is based on the "Bone" series of graphic novels.

At age 13, Mendler started traveling to audition in Los Angeles, which was about 400 miles from her home. Because Los Angeles is the center of the film and entertainment industry, many of the most high-profile jobs are found there. In 2006, shortly after she began auditioning in Los Angeles, Mendler was chosen for a guest role on the daytime TV drama "General Hospital," a long-running and very popular soap opera that is seen nationally.

In 2007, Mendler played Pamela, a minor character in the film *Alice Upside Down,* which starred Alyson Stoner and featured Luke Perry. The story concerns Alice, a shy, adolescent girl whose mother has died. When her father moves with Alice and her brother to a new town, the girl feels even more isolated and out-of-place. She creates a vivid fantasy life for herself, which sometimes gets her into trouble. In addition to having a small on-screen part in the movie, Mendler also performed two songs for the soundtrack, "Free Spirit" and "Frog Prince Song."

In 2008, Mendler appeared as Kristen Gregory in the direct-to-DVD movie *The Clique.* Kristen is part of the self-named "Pretty Committee," a small group of the most popular and fashionable girls at the Octavian Country

Day School. Kristen, an athletic girl, has a secret. She attends Octavian on a scholarship, and her parents are very poor. The clique's leader, Massie, finds her own status at the school threatened when her parents' middle-class friends move into their guest house, bringing along their daughter Claire. The girls of the clique reject Claire at first, but as time passes, she proves to be a true friend. Claire finds out the truth about Kristen's family, but she does not tell the other "Pretty Committee" girls, who would immediately have rejected Kristen if they knew she was not wealthy.

CAREER HIGHLIGHTS

Like many young actors, Mendler hoped to work for Disney. The Disney studios are known for giving selected young actors a chance at huge success. Disney specializes in picking out young, inexperienced performers with potential and then giving them the training, experience, publicity, and opportunity to become famous. Britney Spears, Justin Timberlake, and Miley Cyrus all got their start with Disney. Mendler did a few auditions for Disney, including one for a part in the show "Sonny with a Chance," which went to Demi Lovato instead. Mendler began to get discouraged, but the producers at the Disney studio had really already noticed her. "Bridgit is a great example of … us finding somebody, knowing that we wanted to do business with her and then waiting to find the perfect role," stated Gary Marsh, chief creative officer for Disney Channels Worldwide.

First Appearances on the Disney Channel

Mendler got her first Disney role in 2008. In October 2008, she made a guest appearance on the premiere episode of the program "JONAS," a Disney program featuring the popular singing group the Jonas Brothers. In the show, the brothers played characters much like themselves, siblings who have formed a hit musical group. Mendler played Penny, a girl on whom Nick Jonas's character has a crush. Mendler not only acted in the program, she also had the chance to demonstrate her musical skills, playing a guitar and singing a duet with Nick Jonas. "I was pretty star struck, I'm not going to lie!" she recalled. Once she relaxed, however, she enjoyed working with the Jonas Brothers. "I think it was the first day on set that they brought me into the studio and I started recording the song. So I was a little intimidated but it was really fun," she remembered.

Just a couple of weeks after she finished work on "JONAS," Mendler began work on "Wizards of Waverly Place," a Disney program starring Selena Gomez, David Henrie, and Jake T. Austin as a trio of siblings who are all wizards-in-training. Their father is an ex-wizard, while their mother is a mortal.

Mendler playing a vampire in a scene from the Disney program "Wizards of Waverly Place," with David Henrie and Jake T. Austin.

In addition to needing to keep their magical heritage a secret from the world at large, the siblings have to compete with each other—only one can become the wizard of their generation, and the other two must eventually become mortal. Mendler worked on four episodes of the series initially, playing the part of Juliet Van Heusen, a vampire who is the love interest of Justin, the eldest of the young wizards. Unlike most vampires, Juliet has a soul, and she is considerably nicer than most vampires. She and Justin face the disapproval of their families because of their different backgrounds, but they remain committed to each other. Mendler later returned to the show and appeared in a second round of episodes, still playing the character of Juliet.

Mendler enjoyed working on the program. "I think that the writers on that show are really funny, so that's good," she commented. "The cast and the crew were incredibly welcoming to me, and I felt like I was part of the family when I was on the show."

In addition to her work for Disney, Mendler worked on other projects. She did voice acting again in the animated feature *Alvin and the Chipmunks: The Squeakquel,* supplying the voice of a minor character named Becca. She had a more significant role in the TV movie *Labor Pains,* starring Lindsay Lohan, first broadcast on the ABC Family Channel. Mendler played Emma, the younger sister of Lohan's character Thea Clayhill. Their parents have died, so Thea is the guardian of teenaged Emma. Feeling that she is about to be fired, Thea pretends to be pregnant, thereby gaining her employer's sympathy and holding on to the job that supports her and her sister. *Labor Pains* and *Alvin and the Chipmunks: The Squeakquel* were both released in 2009.

Filming a Pilot

While working on these other projects, Mendler had auditioned for a new show Disney was developing, originally titled "Love, Teddy." Many of Disney's programs include a fantastic element, such as a character's secret life, magical powers, or fabulous wealth. In contrast, this new show, "Love, Teddy," would be more along the lines of the classic TV comedies of the past, featuring a family facing everyday challenges. The people at Disney hoped it would be a program that parents would watch with their children.

The show revolves around two teenaged siblings who find themselves in charge of their infant sister when both of their parents must return to work full-time. Teddy and her older brother PJ cooperate with each other, but in addition to taking care of the baby, they also have to cope with their tween brother Gabe, who feels jealous and insecure about his place in the family. Teddy decides to record a video diary for her sister, with tips and wisdom for surviving in their family. The video segments close each episode, and the title "Love, Teddy" was a reference to the way Teddy ended each of her diary entries to her little sister, Charlie.

For Mendler, the process of auditioning for the show was long. "I was anxiously waiting by the phone for days and days at home," she remembered. "I went into the final audition and then they didn't let me know for, like, a week or two about if I got it or not. You kind of start to lose your confidence the longer [they don't get back to you]. By the end, I was like, 'oh my gosh, will they ever call? Will I know?' I was jumping up and down when I found out I got it."

About a month after finishing up her initial work on "Wizards of Waverly Place," Mendler shot the pilot episode for the program "Love, Teddy." A pilot is a test episode of a program that's being considered for production as a regular series. Depending on how well the pilot is received, the show may go into regular production, or it may be set aside.

"Good Luck Charlie"

By the time Mendler filmed her second batch of appearances on "Wizards of Waverly Place," Disney was ready to go ahead with regular production of "Love, Teddy," now named "Good Luck Charlie." The cast included Mendler as Teddy Duncan, Jason Dolley as PJ, Bradley Steven Perry as

Gabe, Mia Talerico as baby Charlie, and Eric Allan Kramer and Leigh-Allyn Baker as parents Bob and Amy. In addition to starring in the show, Mendler also sang the theme song.

"Teddy's great," Mendler said about her character. "I think in a lot of ways she's just your normal teen girl. She's interested in all the teen girl things. There's an episode where she's into a certain vampire craze; it's like the equivalent of *Twilight.* She's into boys and has her whole teen drama stuff. She's kind of a perfectionist. She likes things to go her way; she likes things to be done right." Reviewing the show for the *Chicago Tribune,* Brian Lowry said that Mendler was "easily the best thing about the sprightly new sitcom 'Good Luck Charlie,' a surprisingly refreshing throwback to ABC's TGIF-style sitcoms."

Discussing Mendler and "Good Luck Charlie" on the web site Radio Free.com, Michael J. Lee wrote, "Any sentimentality in 'Charlie' is usually deftly trumped by a well-balanced moment of disarming humor." He noted that the show allows Mendler a chance to develop a more realistic character than the one she had played in "Wizards of Waverly Place" and called Teddy "a conscientious teen of the internet age who balances her responsibilities at home with the lightheartedness of adolescence." Mendler has said that she appreciates the underlying message in "Good Luck Charlie" that teenagers should take on some adult responsibilities. She's also happy that the message doesn't overpower the episodes' storylines, remaining in the background instead. In addition to the TV program, a movie version of "Good Luck Charlie" is being developed.

> "Teddy's great," Mendler said about her character. "I think in a lot of ways she's just your normal teen girl. She's interested in all the teen girl things. There's an episode where she's into a certain vampire craze; it's like the equivalent of **Twilight**. She's into boys and has her whole teen drama stuff. She's kind of a perfectionist. She likes things to go her way; she likes things to be done right."

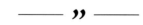

Developing a Musical Career

Many of Disney's TV stars have gone on to have high-powered careers in the music business. Mendler already liked to sing and write songs when she signed a contract with the studio. "I do that for my own fun and so I

Mendler with the cast of "Good Luck Charlie." The Duncan family (from left): Mendler (Teddy), Eric Allan Kramer (Bob), Bradley Steven Perry (Gabe), Mia Talerico (Charlie), Leigh-Allyn Baker (Amy), and Jason Dolley (PJ).

don't think I'm doing it because I'm a part of Disney," she explained. "Hopefully at some point I'll be able to show people my actual songs, maybe put together an album."

Disney periodically releases albums in the "DisneyMania" series, featuring music from the studio's movie soundtracks. A fan of the series, Mendler was excited to be part of *DisneyMania7*. She recorded "When She Loved Me," a song from *Toy Story 2*. "They turned the lights down low in the recording studio and let me do my kind of thing," she remembered. "And I think I was in a good space while I was doing it so I definitely got into the emotions of the song." She was pleased with the results. "I am happy with it. I thought it was a fun song to do and I hope that other people like it too." She also recorded "How to Believe," a song for the Disney DVD feature *Tinkerbell and the Great Fairy Rescue,* released in 2010.

Mendler's singing and acting skills are showcased in the upcoming Disney Channel TV movie *Lemonade Mouth,* based on the book by Mark Peter Hughes. Mendler plays the lead character, Olivia White. Olivia, Mo, Charlie, Stella, and Wen are five high school students who get to know each other when they are all assigned to detention. Alone, they may feel like misfits, but as a group, they start up a rock band that gives them confidence and threatens their school's snobby elite. The movie is scheduled to premier in 2011.

Despite starring in movies and her own TV show, Mendler doesn't take herself too seriously. She says her family helps to keep her down-to-earth. "I trip over everything … I'm a huge klutz," she said. "I'm not cool at all."

FAVORITE BOOKS AND TELEVISION

Mendler enjoys the TV shows "The Office" and "90210," calling the latter her "guilty pleasure." She enjoys "The Twilight Saga" series of books and describes herself as "Team Jacob." Her favorite actress is Natalie Portman.

HOBBIES AND OTHER INTERESTS

Mendler considers herself "a huge nerd. I love reading and math—and I'm really into nerdy dancing. In my book, there's no such thing as a wrong move." She loves music, whether writing it, performing, or just listening. "Every morning when I'm in the car going to work, we'll blast music," she said. "We just jam out. It's a great way to start the day because sometimes, you know, if it's gonna be a stressful day, it's nice to loosen up and have fun." She has a collection of vinyl records and enjoys playing them on her record player. She loves to document things on video and create her own music videos. Her favorite foods are sushi and chocolate.

SELECTED CREDITS

Television

"JONAS," 2009 (guest star)
Labor Pains, 2009 (TV movie)
"Wizards of Waverly Place," 2009-2010 (guest star)
"Good Luck Charlie," 2010-

Movies

The Legend of Buddha, 2004
Alice Upside Down, 2007
The Clique, 2008
Alvin and the Chipmunks: The Squeakquel, 2009

FURTHER READING

Periodicals

Girls' Life, Apr. 1, 2010, p.50

Online Articles

http://www.girlslife.com
   (Girls' Life, "GL Set Visit: Hangin' with Good Luck Charlie's Bridgit
   Mendler," Apr. 2, 2010)
http://www.radiofree.com
   (Radio Free, "Family Antics, Breakthrough Roles, and Wagon Rides: An
   Exclusive Interview with Bridgit Mendler," May 11, 2010)
http://tommy2.net
   (Tommy2.net, "Interview: Bridgit Mendler," undated)

ADDRESS

Bridgit Mendler
Disney Studios
500 South Buena Vista Street
Burbank, CA 91506

WORLD WIDE WEB SITES

http://tv.disney.go.com/disneychannel/goodluckcharlie
http://www.facebook.com

Ryan Sheckler 1989-
American Skateboarder
Youngest-Ever Gold Medal Winner at the X Games

BIRTH

Ryan Allen Sheckler was born on December 30, 1989, in La Palma, California, a small city in the greater Los Angeles area. He was the first of three sons born to Gretchen, who managed a dental office, and Randall (Randy) Sheckler, a mechanical engineer and entrepreneur. His brother Shane was born when he was two, and his brother Kane when he was nine. The brothers grew up in San Clemente, California, a coastal city midway between Los Angeles and San Diego.

YOUTH

Sheckler was a very active child, and he first tried to ride a skateboard at 18 months of age. He had spied his father's skateboard in the garage and ended up riding it on one knee, like a surfboard. When he was young, he said, "Everywhere we went, that was the first thing that came out of the car with me. If we went to the park, I didn't want to play in the sandbox, I just wanted to ride that board." He received his own skateboard at age four and soon learned to perform an ollie, a basic skateboarding trick where the rider pops the tail of the board on the ground to make it jump, then levels the board in the air to land on all four wheels. From that point on, he obsessed over learning new tricks. When he was trying to master the kickflip—an ollie where the board rotates lengthwise before landing—his mother limited him to 100 attempts per day. It took him a year of practicing, but he finally mastered the trick.

> **When he was young, Sheckler said, "Everywhere we went, that was the first thing that came out of the car with me. If we went to the park, I didn't want to play in the sandbox, I just wanted to ride that board."**

When Sheckler was seven, his father rewarded his devoted practice by building a small training ramp in the family's backyard. There were six skate parks near the family's home, including one used by skateboarding pioneer Tony Hawk. (For more information about Hawk, see *Biography Today*, Apr. 2001.) But Sheckler's family built their own, and their "park" eventually grew to include the rails, platforms, and ramps he needed to develop his skills. At age seven, he began competing in the California Amateur Skateboard League, winning every contest he entered during his first year, including the first of five consecutive state championships. Not long after, his mother quit her job to become his manager, scheduling family vacations so that her son could compete around the country. By the time Sheckler was 10, he was attracting sponsors like Oakley sunglasses, Etnies shoes, and Volcom clothes. He frequently finished in the top three at events like the Vans Warped Tour, sometimes even against professionals. By the time he was 13, it was clear Sheckler was ready to compete with the best, and he turned pro in 2003.

EDUCATION

As a professional skateboarder touring the world, Sheckler had little time for school. He was home schooled until he took a brief break from full-time competition to spend his freshman year at San Clemente High School, where he joined the wrestling team. After a year, however, the family decided that he was hurting his career by not competing widely, so he finished his education at Futures Halstrom High School in Mission Viejo, a school for independent study designed for serious young athletes and artists. He attended one-on-one classes twice a week and studied at home or on tour the rest of the time.

CAREER HIGHLIGHTS

Turning Pro

Sheckler's performance in 2003, his first season, soon justified his decision to turn pro. He competed in the park or street divisions of competitions, where skaters are judged on how they navigate a course and perform tricks on and around a series of obstacles. These obstacles could include ramps, boxes, rails, and walls; park competitions had taller ramps and walls, like a skate park, while street competitions were designed more like a real street. Sheckler earned a second place at the Scandinavian Open, then won the Vans Slam City Jam in Vancouver, making him the youngest skateboarder ever to win a professional event. He proved his success wasn't a fluke with additional first place finishes at the Gravity Games and the New Jersey Triple Crown. Two of his wins that year were in the Vans Triple Crown series, and a ninth-place finish in the final competition gave him the overall series title in the street division.

For competitors in action sports like skateboarding and motocross, the annual X Games, sponsored by cable sports network ESPN, is one of the most important competitions in their sport. Sheckler competed in his first X Games in 2003, entering the skateboard park event. He was the only competitor to land every trick he attempted, and he walked away with the gold medal. At 13, he was the youngest competitor ever to win an X Games event, a feat that landed him in the *Guinness Book of World Records.* He later attributed his success to a need to prove himself: "I turned pro that year and was really motivated to win everything I en-tered." Winning the X Games medal, he added, "changed everything. It changed the way I looked at skating because I knew I could hang with the big boys and I could skate." His successes over the year also earned him enough points to be named the year's overall street champion by the World Cup of Skateboarding.

Sheckler also grabbed attention early in his career by creating a signature move. Called the "Shecklair," the move was a kickflip where he grabbed the board between his feet (a move called an indy), but with his legs ex-

*Sheckler competed in the X Games for the first time in 2003,
when he was 13 years old, and won the gold medal in the park event.*

tended. His flair and his early success led to more opportunities. He went on tour with Tony Hawk and was featured in the skating star's video game *Underground 2.* He also got his first real movie work with a small role in the 2003 film *Grind.* Sheckler had been in a movie before, in the 2001 release *MVP: Most Vertical Primate,* in which he worked as a stunt double for a skateboarding monkey. "I thought it was gonna be cool but it turned out kind of stupid," he recalled about having to skate in a monkey suit. In the skating film *Grind,* Sheckler had a small role as a young skateboarder, showing off some of his moves.

Dominating the First Dew Tour

During the 2004 season, Sheckler curbed his competition schedule, skipping everything but major events so he could attend high school like a regular kid. Unlike regular kids, he was earning six figures in competitions, collecting gifts from his sponsors, and being featured on an episode of MTV's "Cribs." He also began performing in skateboarding videos, contributing to Digital Skateboards' *Everyday* video and Almost Skateboards' video *Round Three.* At competitions before the school year started, Sheckler earned a first place at the Vancouver stop of the Vans Triple Crown and a bronze in street at the Gravity Games. Combined with a ninth-place finish in street at the X Games, he placed second overall in the World Cup of Skateboarding street series.

Sheckler returned to full-time competition in the 2005 season, the first year for the Dew Action Sports Tour (AST), a series of five skateboard and motocross competitions. He won the first two events, placed second at the third, and clinched the Dew Cup for street skateboarding by winning the fourth stop. He placed third at the last event, giving him more points than any athlete in any event, earning him the title of Action Sports Tour Athlete of the Year. Besides a bonus of $100,000, Sheckler earned a new Toyota Tacoma truck. At 15, he wasn't even old enough to drive. The victories also earned him another overall street championship from the World Cup of Skateboarding. That year he also made a cameo appearance as himself in the skateboarding movie *Dishdogz.*

The skater kept competing during the 2006 season, earning his second consecutive Dew Cup for park skateboarding. After winning the first stop on the tour, he showed his toughness by competing in the second event only two weeks after severely burning his foot on a hot grill during a beach barbeque. He went on to win the third and fourth Dew AST events and clinched the overall championship with a second-place finish in the final event. He also placed second at the X Games and was awarded Arby's Action Sports Awards for Skateboarder and Athlete of the Year. In 2006 he went on tour again with skateboarding legend Hawk, who told *USA Today* that Sheckler was "arguably one of the best all-around skaters today, probably the best. In terms of versatility, he's the best guy anywhere, and he's only 16." At 16, Sheckler already had a signature sneaker with Etnies, as well as his personal brands of Volcom jeans and eyewear for Oakley. The latter company featured him on its skateboarding video *Our Life* in 2006.

*Sheckler won the Dew Cup in 2005, 2006, and 2007 (shown here)—
the first skater to win it three years in a row.*

The following season Sheckler again made history by becoming the first skater to win the Dew Action Sports Tour championship three years in a row. He won three events and placed second in the other two competitions, running away with the skate park title with 450 out of a possible 500 points. He also placed fourth at the street event at the 2007 X Games. As a teenager, Sheckler was living a life other kids could only dream about: traveling the world to competitions, attending celebrity parties and events like the MTV Video Awards, and earning a considerable income, as well as loads of free gifts from sponsors. "A part of me relates to kids my age, a part of me doesn't," he noted. "I'm not complaining about my life, but it definitely gets to me when I want to go to the beach. But then, I also want to travel and do all these cool things I get to do. It kind of clashes a little bit, but it's not something I can't handle."

Starring in a Hit Reality TV Show

Executives at MTV were intrigued with Sheckler's hectic lifestyle, and they asked to make a reality show out of his life. "Life of Ryan" debuted in fall 2007 and became MTV's best-rated new series that season, with 41 million viewers watching its eight episodes. While viewers were treated to glimpses of Sheckler traveling and competing, they mostly saw him dealing with the same issues other teens face: finding a girlfriend, managing his friendships, and, most prominently, dealing with his parents' recent divorce. "After years of commoners' showboating, here comes a showboat who wants to be common," critic Ned Martel noted in the *New York Times.* The reviewer added that the reality show was worth watching because Sheckler "is good at something and still manages to be humble yet charismatic, ambitious yet magnanimous, hard-working yet fun-loving."

"Life of Ryan" continued for 21 more episodes over two seasons; Sheckler cut the third season short after six episodes because he felt it was taking away from his skateboarding. After his show took off, he got criticism from some skaters for "selling out" and taking skateboarding into the mainstream. He became one of the few skateboarding stars to appear in ads for non-skating products, including Axe body spray and Panasonic electronics, and some critics believed he was harming the sport by dulling its edge. Sheckler took the criticism in stride: "All I can do is focus on the positives, man.... Skating is a blessing and that's all I want to do. People can say what they want. I don't think negative anymore. It's too hard. Positivity will take you way further." The show brought plenty of positives to his life, including lots of fans who were new to skateboarding. Groups of screaming teenage girls became a common sight at his competitions.

Skateboarding legend Tony Hawk said that Sheckler is "arguably one of the best all-around skaters today, probably the best. In terms of versatility, he's the best guy anywhere, and he's only 16."

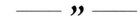

Sheckler continued winning titles during the 2008 season. He picked up wins in the first and third events on the Dew Tour, as well as a second place at the fourth event; non-podium finishes in the other two events meant he finished third overall in skate park. He bounced back by earning his second X Games gold medal in 2008, placing first in street skateboarding despite competing with a broken elbow. He counted his first place at *Thrasher* magazine's Bust or Bail contest, in which competitors worked a rail on a set of 17 stairs, as one of his best victories. In 2008 he also worked on a video for sponsor Red Bull with his skateboarding friends and idols, arranging many of the film's events and taking the group to sites in Dubai and Australia. That year he also began branching out with an apparel line, helping to design his own shoe for Etnies and expanding his clothing line. He partnered with department store JC Penney to release a whole line casual wear, called RS by Sheckler. He helped design the line, which included jeans, T-shirts, shorts, and hoodies.

*Sheckler in his trophy room, in a scene from the
MTV reality show "Life of Ryan."*

In 2008, Sheckler created the Sheckler Foundation with his brothers to give back to the community. They sponsored an annual golf tournament, the Sheckler Foundation Celebrity Skins Classic, to raise money for a variety of causes. They partnered with several other charities, including the Make-A-Wish Foundation and groups supporting research into autism and spinal cord injuries. Other partners included a group that provided funds to help injured action athletes and the Rob Dyrdek Foundation, which helped promote skateboarding, especially to kids in underprivileged communities. "I feel really blessed to be involved in those things," Sheckler said. "I feel like I am supposed to give back. I have a responsibility to do more than just skateboard and sit around."

Coming Back from Injury

Sheckler had reconstructive surgery on his elbow in 2009, then returned to competition. He took first in the Skate Open ISF Skateboarding World Championships, the first event in the Dew Tour. At that year's X Games, however, he broke his foot during one of his runs, forcing him to sit out the rest of the season. Getting hurt has been part of being a professional skater, and over the course of his career Sheckler has also suffered a fractured foot, broken elbows (five times), and concussions (three times). "I got all these other scars from skating, but it's my life, dude," he said. "I absolutely love it. I am always hurt but what are you going to do? I have to skate." The foot injury kept him out of action for five months, but he kept busy with his growing acting career. He appeared in the 2009 film *Street Dreams* as the rival and friend of a young man trying to make it as a pro skater.

Sheckler took his first non-skating acting role with the 2010 comedy *The Tooth Fairy*, which starred Dwayne "The Rock" Johnson. Sheckler played Mick, a hockey player and teammate of Johnson's character, who is transformed into a tooth fairy. For the role, Sheckler learned to ice skate so he could perform all but the worst falls in his scenes. The experience was interesting enough that he said he would be open to other non-skateboarding acting roles: "I'll always have my skate life, but I absolutely like the fun of making movies."

After spending long months away from skating, Sheckler was eager to return. "I think that coming back into skateboarding is going to feel like the best thing that's ever happened to me," he remarked. He rejoined the Dew Tour, now consisting of four events, for the 2010 season. He followed a second-place finish at the first stop with two thirds and a fourth, ending up second overall on the Tour. At the X Games that summer he earned his third gold medal, clinching the skateboard street event with a near-perfect run. He also participated in the first season of skateboard entrepreneur Rob Dyrdek's Street League DC Pro Tour, a new series of competitions designed to feature the best skateboarders competing for a record $1.2 million in prize money. The new format instantly scored tricks as riders navigated the course, allowing riders and fans to see the success of each trick. Although Sheckler's best finish at the three events was only a fourth place, he did notch the highest scoring single trick of the series. With the tour offering revenue sharing to participating skaters, Sheckler was prepared to continue with the tour in 2011, even though it meant he might have to give up other tournaments.

Competing against the best skaters appealed to him, Sheckler said. "I like the competition because it keeps me mentally focused on something besides learning a trick or linking tricks together. I'm always trying to figure out ways to one up everyone and that's what I love about competitions. I love challenging myself and pushing the envelope." He maintained good relationships with his fellow skaters, however, and felt honored when he was asked to join the skating team of Plan B skateboards. He toured with skaters like multiple X Games winner Paul Rodriguez and video stars Torey Pudwill and P. J. Ladd, and collaborated on the Plan B video *Superfuture*. "You know, we're competitors but we're all friends—really good friends—so ... it's nice to be in a place where it feels like we can all respect each

*After a tough injury in 2009, Sheckler came back
and earned a gold medal in the street event at the 2010 X Games.*

other and respect what we're doing and respect mutual accomplishments," he explained.

Sheckler was surprised in 2010 when he won the Kids' Choice Award for favorite male athlete over basketball stars Kobe Bryant and LeBron James and snowboarder/skateboarder Shaun White. He attributed his growing popularity and continuing success to hard work. "People think this life was just handed to me. But I started from ground zero like everybody else," he said. "I have been doing tricks since I was six years old. I was focused and determined from that long ago. That's why I am where I am." He credited his family and his Christian faith for keeping him grounded and away from potential troubles with drinking or drugs. "I always skated for myself and just wanted to be good for myself," he explained. "Any pressure is only me wanting to succeed and pushing myself to do so."

Sheckler continues to push himself as an athlete. He has begun working with a personal trainer to keep himself fit for competition, improving his stamina by biking or swimming nearly every day. A sponsor helped him build his own private two-story skate park for practicing his skating skills. He knows he can't skate forever, and he's thought about staying involved in the business side of skating after he retires. But for now, he has goals he still wants to achieve in the sport. He said his dream accomplishment would be earning *Thrasher* magazine's Skater of the Year, an award that is voted on by skateboarding's most hard-core fans. He thought he had the potential to achieve this goal, even if it took years. "I still don't know my boundaries," he acknowledged, "and I've been skating professionally since I was 13." Sheckler was once asked how he will know he's reached his ultimate goal—to be one of the best skaters ever. "I want to make a huge contribution to skateboarding," he replied. "The only way I will know that I have achieved legendary status is when my peers say I have. There is no other way."

HOME AND FAMILY

When Sheckler turned 18, he bought his own house and began living on his own. His house was close to both parents in San Clemente, California, so he could spend as much time as possible with his younger brothers and friends. In 2010 he got his first pet, a little dog he named Dollar.

HOBBIES AND OTHER INTERESTS

Away from skateboarding, Sheckler enjoys other action sports, including surfing, snowboarding, and riding dirt bikes. He also enjoys music and movies. In addition to his work with the Sheckler Foundation, the skater is quick to get involved in other charitable activities. He has skated with sick children for the Make-A-Wish Foundation, and in 2008 he donated his Range Rover to be auctioned for the Children's Cancer Research Fund, raising almost $200,000.

SELECTED CREDITS

Television
"Life of Ryan," 2007-08

Skateboarding Videos
Everyday, 2004
Round Three, 2004
Our Life, 2006
Tony Hawk's Secret Skatepark Tour, Vol. 2, 2006
Slaughter at the Opera, 2008

Movies
MVP: Most Vertical Primate, 2001 (stunt double)
Grind, 2003
Dishdogz, 2005 (as himself)
Street Dreams, 2009
The Tooth Fairy, 2010

HONORS AND AWARDS
Vans Triple Crown Overall Street Champion: 2003
Gold Medal in Skateboard Park (Summer X Games): 2003
Overall Street Champion (World Cup of Skateboarding): 2003 and 2005
Athlete of the Year (Dew Action Sports Tour): 2005
Dew Cup in Skateboard Park (Dew Action Sports Tour): 2005, 2006, 2007
Skateboarder and Athlete of the Year (Arby's Action Sports Awards): 2006
Gold Medal in Skateboard Street (Summer X Games): 2008, 2010
Kids' Choice Award (Nickelodeon): 2010, for Favorite Male Athlete
Teen Choice Award: 2010, for Choice Action Sports Athlete

FURTHER READING

Books
Nicholas, Kimberly, *Ryan Sheckler: The Real Life of a Hot Skater,* 2008

Periodicals
Denver Post, July 8, 2005, p.D10

Los Angeles Times, Oct. 5, 2000, p.1; July 20, 2004, p.D1; Oct. 14, 2006, p.D10
Miami Herald, Oct. 16, 2006
New York Times, Sep. 20, 2006, p.A1; Jan. 22, 2008, p.8
Sports Illustrated for Kids, Jan. 2004, p.52; Aug. 2008, p.18
Thrasher, Apr. 2004, p.156
Transworld Skateboarding, Aug. 2006, p.146; Apr. 2008, p.156
USA Today, July 10, 2006, p.C12; July 2, 2008, p.C2

Online Articles

http://espn.go.com/action
   (ESPN, "A League of Their Own," June 3, 2010; "Candid Conversation:
   Ryan Sheckler," Dec. 9, 2009; "Catching up with Ryan Sheckler," Dec. 9,
   2009; "Checking in with Ryan Sheckler," May 19, 2010; "Just Another
   Lonely Millionaire Skateboarder," July 16, 2008)
http://sportsillustrated.cnn.com
   (Sports Illustrated, "Q&A with Ryan Sheckler," Aug. 1, 2009)

ADDRESS

Ryan Sheckler
Ryan Sheckler, Inc.
111 Del Cabo
San Clemente, CA 92673

WORLD WIDE WEB SITE

http://www.ryansheckler.com

Photo and Illustration Credits

Front Cover Photos: Robert Bullard: Courtesy of Robert D. Bullard; Angelina Jolie: Movie still: THE TOURIST Photo by Peter Mountain © 2010 Columbia Pictures/ Sony Publicity. All Rights Reserved; Charles Martinet (Mario): ar/Newscom; Ryan Sheckler: Kevin Novak/CSM/Landov.

Robert Bullard/Photos: AP Photo/Ric Feld (p. 9); David Rae Morris/Bloomberg via Getty Images (p. 12); Book cover: DUMPING IN DIXIE: Race, Class, and Environmental Quality by Robert D. Bullard © 1990, 1994, 2000 Westview Press/Perseus Book Group (p. 14); AP Photo/Ric Feld (p. 17); Courtesy of Robert D. Bullard (p. 19).

Paula Creamer/Photos: Jonathan Ferrey/Getty Images (p. 23); Icon Sports Media 356/Icon SMI/Newscom (p. 27); AP Photo/Daytona Beach News-Journal/William Dunkley (p. 29); AP Photo/Mike Groll (p. 32).

Lucas Cruikshank/Photos: Mark Davis/PictureGroup via AP Images (p. 35); PRNews Foto/ContentNext Media/Newscom (p. 37); Vivian Zink/Disney Channel via Getty Images (p. 40); Movie still: FRED: THE MOVIE © 2010 Lionsgate Home Entertainment (p. 42).

Jason Derülo/Photos: Angela Weiss/Getty Images (p. 45); Larry Marano/Getty Images (p. 48); CD cover: WHATCHA SAY © 2010 Beluga Heights/Warner Bros. (p. 51); PictureGroup/MTV (p. 53).

Angelina Jolie/Photos: SPE, Inc./Santiago Gonzalez Sanchez © 2010 Columbia Pictures/Sony. All Rights Reserved. (p. 57); Movie still/DVD: GEORGE WALLACE 2009 © Warner Home Video. All Rights Reserved. (p. 60, top); Movie still: HACKERS Photo by Mark Tillie/United Artists Pictures, Inc. (via Movie Goods) © 1995 All Rights Reserved. (p. 60, middle); Movie Still/DVD: GIRL, INTERRUPTED © 1999 Global Entertainment Production GmbH & Co. Movie KG. All Rights Reserved. Distributed by Columbia Pictures/Sony Home Entertainment (p. 60, bottom); Movie still: LARA CROFT: TOMB RAIDER © 2001 Paramount (via Movie Goods). All Rights Reserved. (p. 62); UNHCR via Getty Images (p. 64); Movie still: KUNG FU PANDA © 2008 Dreamworks Animated (via Movie Goods) (p. 67); Movie still: THE TOURIST Photo by Peter Mountain © 2010 Columbia Pictures/Sony Publicity. All Rights Reserved. (p. 69); AP Photo/UNHCR/Aziz (p. 71).

Monica Lozano/Photos: La Opinión Photos/Newscom (p. 75); Los Angeles Daily News Negatives. Part of Department of Special Collections, Charles E. Young Research Library, University of California at Los Angeles, ID: uclalat_1387_b37_24570-1 (p. 77); J. Emilio Flores/La Opinión/Newscom (p. 81); Aurelia Ventura/La Opinión/Newscom (p. 83); Larry Downing/Reuters/Landov (p. 85).

Cumulative Names Index

This cumulative index includes the names of all individuals profiled in *Biography Today* since the debut of the series in 1992.

For cumulative general, places of birth, and birthday indexes, please see biographytoday.com

For cumulative general, places of birth, and birthday indexes, please see biographytoday.com.

165

For cumulative general, places of birth, and birthday indexes, please see biographytoday.com

For cumulative general, places of birth, and birthday indexes, please see biographytoday.com

Biography Today

General Series

Biography Today **General Series** includes a unique combination of current biographical profiles that teachers and librarians — and the readers themselves — tell us are most appealing. The **General Series** is available as a 3-issue subscription; hardcover annual cumulation; or subscription plus cumulation.

Within the **General Series**, your readers will find a variety of sketches about:

- Authors
- Musicians
- Political leaders
- Sports figures
- Movie actresses & actors
- Cartoonists
- Scientists
- Astronauts
- TV personalities
- and the movers & shakers in many other fields!

ONE-YEAR SUBSCRIPTION

- 3 softcover issues, 6" x 9"
- Published in April, April, and September
- 1-year subscription, list price $66. **School and library price $64**
- 150 pages per issue
- 10 profiles per issue
- Contact sources for additional information
- Cumulative Names Index

HARDBOUND ANNUAL CUMULATION

- Sturdy 6" x 9" hardbound volume
- Published in December
- List price $73. **School and library price $66 per volume**
- 450 pages per volume
- 30 profiles — includes all profiles found in softcover issues for that calendar year
- Cumulative General Index, Places of Birth Index, and Birthday Index

SUBSCRIPTION AND CUMULATION COMBINATION

- $110 for 3 softcover issues plus the hardbound volume

For Cumulative General, Places of Birth, and Birthday Indexes, please see www.biographytoday.com.

"*Biography Today* will be useful in elementary and middle school libraries and in public library children's collections where there is a need for biographies of current personalities. High schools serving reluctant readers may also want to consider a subscription."
— *Booklist,* American Library Association

"Highly recommended for the young adult audience. Readers will delight in the accessible, energetic, tell-all style; teachers, librarians, and parents will welcome the clever format [and] intelligent and informative text. It should prove especially useful in motivating 'reluctant' readers or literate nonreaders."
— *MultiCultural Review*

"Written in a friendly, almost chatty tone, the profiles offer quick, objective information. While coverage of current figures makes *Biography Today* a useful reference tool, an appealing format and wide scope make it a fun resource to browse." — *School Library Journal*

"The best source for current information at a level kids can understand."
— Kelly Bryant, School Librarian, Carlton, OR

"Easy for kids to read. We love it! Don't want to be without it."
— Lynn McWhirter, School Librarian, Rockford, IL